Weightless

Healing from an Eating Disorder

JESSICA LUNN

1ˢᵗ edition 2022
Independently published

Cover design by: KUHN Design Group | kuhndesigngroup.com

ISBN: 9798364348913

To all my friends and family who always believed in me and never gave up hope, and to my mom, for everything.

Also, special credit to my aunt, Tara, and friend Mindy who has helped me in more ways than I can ever express.

DISCLAIMER

This book is not intended to replace individual medical advice or instruction. No action should be taken based solely on the contents of this book, and readers should seek appropriate advice and help from a medical professional in the case of need on any matter related to their health and wellbeing. Although I am a nurse, I have no knowledge of your individual health circumstances and my words are not to be construed as personal advice. I cannot prescribe for you nor answer individual medical enquiries. The information and opinions provided here are believed to be accurate and sound based on the best judgment available, but any action taken as a result of reading this book is taken at the risk of the reader.

AUTHOR'S NOTE

This book encompasses depression, addiction, mental illness, eating disorders, sarcasm, hope, growth, transformation, and experience. It is about the darkest moments of my life, my journey through them, and how I am trying to heal. It is meant to inspire others, yet also validate others' experiences to make them feel less alone.

I wrote this book to educate support systems, medical professionals, and hopefully even provide insight and hope to those suffering from any struggle in life.

I am not a licensed therapist or psychologist, licensed registered dietician, or even a well-known writer (yet?). I am, however, a genuine, honest person who chose a career in helping others. I earned my bachelor's degree in nursing (BSN) and have spent most of my career working in the emergency department. Over the years, I have noticed uncompassionate, unempathetic, and just plain bad medical treatment for those with mental illnesses. As a medical professional and as an expert chronic, difficult, sometimes defiant, ill patient, I feel like I can help at least a few people in this world. Even if I help one person, then my job is done!

Eating disorders are an especially competitive disorder. Competitive in countless ways, even ways that might seem trivial. The focus of this book is not to define an eating disorder as such, or to go into its complications—there are plenty of other books on that and my aim here is to reach out and hopefully touch the hearts of those who are still suffering, and to provide insight to family and friends who must watch their loved one struggle with this truly life destroying disorder. As a nurse and patient both, I also hope to bridge the gap that sometimes exists between the medical profession and those it cares for. As a healthcare professional, I have worked with very sick people, and believe me, I have also been in the position of being desperately ill and in urgent need of receiving care. These two roles combined give me, I believe, a special, even privileged outlook on what it means to experience an eating disorder. In this book, I will not mention weights or calories relating to me or other disordered individuals. Behaviors are mentioned only as necessary because it is not relevant. I am trying to create a supportive, not competitive environment.

This book is in three parts—living with an eating disorder (lotus), recovery and rebirth (phoenix), and living life to its fullest (dragonfly). I have chosen to include some of my poetry to open each section, using different metaphors, taken from nature and mythology, as well as other poems, to express different facets of my recovery. I personally have found that poetry explores and contextualizes aspects of my recovery not easily put into words otherwise, and has high therapeutic value. I am also planning to publish a book of poems that represent the emotions, thoughts, inspirations, and resilience of surviving through an eating disorder. I hope you enjoy this extra dimension to my work!

CONTENTS

PART ONE

Starting from the Mud

THE LOTUS

The purity, inner strength, and tranquility
That I represent do not come easy or at a fair price.
I find myself in dark murky water
And anchor my roots into the mud at the bottom of a pool of dirty liquid.
Slowly, I overcome all the adversities that barricade my path to the surface.
I stay true to myself and continue to strive upwards.
After about two years,
I rise above the dismal environment
And blossom one petal at a time.
This represents the gradual steps in my personal progress.
My flower only emerges in the morning,
And then at night, I disappear back into the murky water
Only to re-emerge again as a new flower the next morning.
Every day I resurrect and start with a new beginning.
I do not fear the dark,
For I know that even in the darkest of nights,
The sun will rise again.

JML

BE A LOTUS

"You must go through darkness to finally see the light."

JESSICA LUNN

L otus flowers. They grow from a bed of murky water and mud. Slowly, over time, they sprout up towards the surface of the water and eventually blossom into a beautiful flower. Their journey is not easy. They start off in the darkness, but nonetheless, they keep reaching for the light until they finally feel the warmth of the sun rays beaming down on them. When I think about lotus flowers, I think about life. Let's be real, life is hard. Many of us find ourselves embedded in the mud of murky water and have to slowly climb up toward the surface to find the light. It isn't an easy task, but it can be done, especially with the support of others and a little bit of hope.

If you are at a point in your life where you do not feel that you can hold the hope for yourself, please understand that there is someone else out there holding it for you. They will hold it for you until you are ready to take it and hold it for yourself. For a long time (it only took me about 20 years to figure this out), I could not see this. Two decades later, I am finally able to hold some hope for myself and for others.

My life experiences have taught me many lessons and have also given me a different perspective on my life and on that of others. Don't get me wrong, my life is by no means perfect, and I still have a considerable amount of painful, difficult work to do. But, a start has been made and I am on my way. When I want to quit, give up, and walk away, I remind myself that I am not travelling this journey only for myself (although if I was, that's okay too!). If my pain helps at least one person, or makes one person feel less alone, then my quest to the surface of that murky water, despite all obstacles, is worth it.

When I became a nurse, I took an oath to follow the four ethical principles of nursing. One, nonmaleficence, or to do no harm. Two, beneficence, or to do the greater good. Three, justice, always to be kind and compassionate towards others despite race, religion, ethnicity, or gender. Four, autonomy, to allow patients the right to make informed decisions about their own medical care, by advocating for the patient, educating them, informing them of risks and benefits, and respecting their health care decisions.[1] Nurse or not, I will always uphold these oaths because that is what everyone deserves. In fact, this is one of the reasons why I chose to write this book. Greater knowledge means greater freedom to choose and act, and, by sharing my own information in this way, I hope to enhance people's ability to make good, informed decisions. Even people who have made poor decisions, though, or who have acted badly, deserve compassion. If you had asked me a year ago, maybe even a month ago, if "bad people" deserve compassion, I would have written a different story. I have since come to terms with the power of compassion, which is truly mind-broadening. Thoughts can change; they are not permanent.

When you cannot forgive the people in your life who have hurt you, you continue to give them power over you. They do not deserve to hold that power over you and you do not deserve to let them! When you hold onto grudges and blame, you remain stuck. Forgiveness will get you unstuck. Forgiveness does not take away the hurt or the suffering, nor does it invalidate your experiences, it simply gives you back the power that was taken away from you. It has taken me a lifetime to learn this, and is still something of which I have to remind myself.

I never thought I would be able to forgive the people who tore my soul apart, but I was wrong. If I can learn to forgive, then so can you. Not that this is simple, it's far from it. It is a lengthy and arduous task; in fact, it will probably be one of the hardest things you do in life. It takes a lot of effort, perseverance, willingness, and self-compassion to forgive; however, I can assure you that it will be freeing. Freedom from mental anguish is one of the best gifts you can give yourself. So, if you or a loved one are feeling broken, I am here to tell you there is nothing you need to fix; you just need to let yourself grow. Be a lotus.

I have thought long and hard about how I wanted to tell my story, how to talk about my life with an eating disorder, my life experiences, and my rocky climb toward something like recovery. Nothing I wrote ever seemed to capture what I wanted to express, or to paint a "Picasso" of my life, so to speak, which would encapsulate and portray everything I wanted to say in one go. One picture is worth a thousand words, as the saying goes, and that is one of the reasons I love art. I wanted my "painted" life to project a certain image and message, that everyone would be able to see with minimal self-interpretation.

Weightless

It was naive of me! Writing down every single detail does not necessarily make a good story. I came to realize that you need selection as well, and, fundamentally, emotional honesty. I realized that if I stayed true to myself and spoke from the heart, then the rest would follow. Why be so formal and literal, when being genuine can reach an audience just as well, if not better? Humans want to feel validated; we want to feel we can relate to someone else. We need the connection. It provides comfort.

⌒∽⌒

Are you wondering about the person writing these words and future words that you will read? I would be. When I began writing this book, I was a 31-year-old magenta-haired woman seated on an uncomfortable airplane seat, flying home from a treatment center that had just banned me from accessing any further help. Go me! After having to leave what was my ninth treatment center, and feeling completely misunderstood, I knew I needed a way to help the system change. I had made mistakes while in treatment and had been resistant to change at times, but leaving treatment was also a systematic chain of errors outside of my control.

I endured numerous difficulties throughout my childhood and adult years, and unfortunately, those past difficulties have significantly affected me. They continue to influence me in current situations, and will probably still be there in future situations. I've had eating disorder thoughts and behaviors since I was around 11 years old, but was not formally diagnosed with anorexia nervosa until I was around 15 or 16. That was when I entered treatment for the first time. I did not realize how ill I really was and told myself that I would be going to a place like a "camp" for a month. Little did I know it was more like boot camp! I lived at that particular facility for approximately four months and continued my education online on the days I was given the opportunity to do school work. I did not take treatment as seriously as I should have, but at the time, I did not understand my disorder or why this was happening to me. I just wanted to feel better, and the only way I knew how to do this was to starve and injure myself.

Looking back, I wish that I had gone into the treatment more deeply— then maybe I would not have turned into a severe chronic case. Maybe I could have saved myself all the pain, suffering, and trauma of eating disorder treatment and hospital stays if I had made more of an effort to understand what was going on? In my defense, however, I was a teenager with minimal insight to my disorder, and how many teenagers are wise enough to understand that adult decisions and actions are sometimes for their own good? I also suffered from anosognosia (a neurological condition whereby you are unable to perceive or be aware of your own illness, see next chapter, *What is an eating disorder*). Today, after nine treatment admissions and one admission to drug detox over the years, I have gained incredible insight into myself, my disorder, and the whole mental health system. This hard-earned hindsight is something I want to share with you. I cannot go back and change the past, but I can learn from it and use that knowledge to help myself and others in the future.

I say that I am "just" a 31-year-old woman trying to write her first book, but I am so much more than that. I am an artist, an emergency room nurse, a writer, a friend, a sister, a daughter, an amazing dog mom to Henry, and a Hufflepuff (any Harry Potter fans here?) Thank you, that's true. A very wise, genuine, caring, authentic, and amazing woman told me and the other patients that we had to say,

"Thank you, that's true", whenever we received a compliment. At first, I thought it was weird, but it does have a nice ring to it, and now I use it all the time!

Now that you know who I am, I am going to tell you who I am not. I am not my eating disorder, my drug addiction, my trauma, my anxiety, or my depression. These are all maladies I battle against on a daily basis, but they do not define who I am. Nobody should define themselves by their inner demons. A cancer patient does not introduce themselves as, "Hi, I am cancer", so why should people with mental illnesses go around and say "Hi, I'm anorexic and a drug addict"?

Many people, including myself, form their identity around their problems. If you identify with this, I invite you to step out of the box. These demons that you and I face every day are just that, demons. You are not your inner demons. It is very important to remind yourself of that. Defining yourself in terms of your condition constitutes an injustice to yourself. Unfortunately, it is a difficult cycle to break, but it can be done!

Numerous times I have asked myself why my life has turned out the way it has. It is okay to have some self-pity, but do not dwell in it, it will only prevent you from becoming that lotus. The question is not, "Why has my life turned out like this?", but rather, "This is where I am at right now, where can I go from here?" I would never wish the hardships I have gone through on anyone else, yet I am thankful for all of the good, bad, and ugly experiences. If someone asked me if I would go back in time and change the outcome of my future, honestly, I would state that I wouldn't change a thing... except for maybe some of those awful yearly school pictures!

My personal story has shaped me into the person I am today. I am able to identify the value in the things that I might not have valued before. My experiences have created a more empathetic entity, possibly made me a more compassionate nurse than I would have been originally, and have given me wisdom beyond my years.

It is difficult to explain what it is like to live inside a brain that only knows eating disorders, addiction, and other co-morbidities. People can empathize with me, but unless they have gone through my exact experiences, they will never know how it truly feels. I have included journal entries, poems, and personal experiences in addition to research and education to express what I cannot express in other ways. The intent is to create insight and understanding... to show you how I started from the mud and made my way up to the surface to blossom, just as you can.

WHAT IS AN
EATING DISORDER?

A n eating disorder is an all-consuming mental disorder with dangerous physical effects. It's not someone messing about with their meals for a bit of drama or attention—it has much more to do with the mind than with food itself. It is torture, no fun, and has potentially devastating consequences. Except for opioid overdose, eating disorders have the highest mortality rate of any mental illness. An estimated one person dies every 52 minutes as a direct result of their illness and its complications—that's 10,200 deaths a year in the United States.[2] According to ACUTE Center for Eating Disorders & Severe Malnutrition, Denver, USA, patients with anorexia nervosa (AN) are five times more likely to die prematurely due to medical complications and 18 times more likely to die from suicide.[3] Bulimia nervosa (BN), has a mortality rate of approximately 3.9% and those affected are also at a higher risk of suicide.[4]

Most people have heard of anorexia, bulimia, and binge eating disorder (BED). However, there are several more types of disorders less known to the community, or which receive less exposure. These other disorders include avoidant restrictive food intake disorder (ARFID), pica (the urge to eat non-food items such as dirt or earth), other specified feeding and eating disorders (OSFED), and rumination disorder (regurgitating food after eating.) The Diagnostic and Statistical Manual of Mental Disorders (DSM-V) provide the criteria for diagnosis of all mental health issues. I believe that the DSM-V can be useful for providers as a diagnostic tool, but also harmful, in that it can prevent people from getting a full course of treatment. Not only is it a diagnostic tool, but a tool for insurance companies to determine when to stop coverage. In treatment, I have seen several people admit (very disordered and unhealthy) and get discharged a week and a half later due to insurance stating they do not meet the weight criteria. A week of treatment is not helpful for anybody, in my opinion. Having a "normal" weight does not mean the eating disorder suddenly went away. It is a mental disease, not a weight disease!

The most recent version of the DSM-V, has made several positive changes to the diagnostic criteria for specific eating disorders, for example, binge eating disorder (BED) is now considered its own diagnosis. In addition, the weight criteria of less than 85% ideal body weight for AN or anorexia changed to "significant low weight".[5]

My biggest issue as a patient, is that the DSM-V now determines the severity of AN by their BMI (BMI of >17 is mild whereas a BMI of >16 is moderate and BMI >15 is severe to extreme). In addition, the DSM-V defines the severity of bulimia by frequency of binge/purge episodes.[6] Yes, weight and/or frequency can help determine the extent of the eating disorder, although it does not determine the severity of the mental aspect of the disease. It is by definition a mental illness and numbers alone cannot describe pathology inside someone's head! Severe or mild, that person still needs and deserves help.

Below is a table giving definitions of different eating disorders and how they may present.

Table 1—Eating disorders and common presentation

EATING DISORDER	COMMON PRESENTATIONS [7,8]
Anorexia nervosa • Obsessive fear of gaining weight and distorted body image • Restrictive type—person significantly restricts food intake to lose weight or maintain a low weight • Purging type—person engages in same behaviors of restricting type but also engages in binges eating and/or purging behaviors • Typically, labs can show as normal, even in severe cases, with the exception of purging type	• Repeated weighing oneself • Significant weight loss or low body weight • Food rituals, food obsession • Preoccupation of weight, calories, numbers, etc • Makes excuses to avoid eating or denies hunger • Excessive and compulsive exercise • Denial of severity • Low self-esteem, high levels of anxiety and depression, and isolation • Extreme mood lability • Control issues, sleep difficulties • Pale/yellow skin tone along with brittle nails and thin, dry hair. • Dizziness, fainting, cold intolerance • Purging behaviors (vomiting, laxatives, diet pills) • Death

Weightless

EATING DISORDER	COMMON PRESENTATIONS[7,8]
Bulimia nervosa • The person regularly engages in binge eating and purging behaviors to compensate the binge eating • Purging behaviors include self-induced vomiting, laxative abuse, excessive exercise, taking diet pills or diuretics, or misusing insulin, typically inhibiting amount of insulin to result in weight loss. (In people with type 1 diabetes, this is called diabulimia, or type 1 diabetes with disordered eating and is highly dangerous) • For DSM diagnosis, behaviors must occur at least once a week for three months or longer • Person may engage in self-injury, substance abuse, and impulsive actions	• Has calluses on the back of the hands and knuckles from self-induced vomiting (Russel's sign) • Dental problems, such as enamel erosion, cavities, discoloration of teeth from vomiting, and tooth sensitivity • Chronically inflamed and sore throat • Swollen salivary (parotid) glands in the neck and jaw area • Acid reflux disorder and other gastrointestinal problems • Intestinal distress and irritation from laxative abuse • Severe dehydration from purging of fluids • Electrolyte imbalance (too low or too high levels of sodium, calcium, potassium, and other minerals) which can lead to stroke or heart attack • Frequent visits to the bathroom after meals • Weight fluctuations • Death

EATING DISORDER	COMMON PRESENTATIONS[7,8]
Binge eating disorder • Most common disorder • Includes reoccurring episode of eating excessive quantities of food in a short time frame with feelings of loss of control. • Does not include compensatory behaviors for the binge	• Following binge episodes, person may have significant distress followed by feelings of shame, guilt, and depression. • Can cause weight gain, is associated with high blood pressure, high cholesterol, type 2 diabetes and heart disease • Eating until uncomfortably full • Eating alone or in secret to avoid embarrassment • Frequently dieting, possibly without weight loss • Low self-esteem • Hiding food • High levels of anxiety/depression • Death
Avoidant restrictive food intake disorder (ARFID) also known as "selective eating disorder" • Person generally has a lack of interest in food and is not associated with weight or appearance • Avoids specific foods due to sensory issues or adverse experience (fear of choking, fear of vomiting, or allergic reaction) • Person is unable to meet their body's nutritional requirements	• Lack of interest in food or eating, low appetite • Extreme pickiness • Social isolation • Anxiety around fear foods, vomiting or gagging after exposure to fear food • Dependence on feeding tube or nutritional supplements • Avoidance/food refusal due to sensory issue or adverse/fear-based experience • Growth failure in children, weight loss in adults • Death
Pica • Abnormal craving for non-foods	• Involves eating items that are not typically thought of as food such as hair, dirt, and paint

EATING DISORDER	COMMON PRESENTATIONS[7,8]
Other specified feeding and eating disorders (OSFED) • Person may in engage in behaviors of anorexia, bulimia, or BED but do not meet the full requirement for a specific diagnosis • Disorders that fall in this category include atypical anorexia, bulimia and BED at low frequency/time criteria, purging disorder, and night eating syndrome • Just because they do not meet the specific criteria of another diagnosis in the DSM, it does not mean it is any less dangerous	• Atypical anorexia—person presents like anorexia except does not meet weight requirement • Bulimia and BED—person does not meet the frequency or time frame designated in the DSM • Purging disorder—purging in the absence of binge eating to influence weight or shape • Night eating syndrome—recurrent episodes of night eating during sleep or after awakening from sleep
Rumination disorder • Regurgitating food after eating	• Regular regurgitation of food. Regurgitated food is re-chewed, re-swallowed, or spit out. • Typically, sufferers do not appear to be making an effort, appear to be stressed, upset, or disgusted by their behaviors.

ANOSOGNOSIA

There is one additional symptom that I would like to discuss. Eating disorders (Eds) significantly affect the structure of the brain and a person's thought process. For example, they can disrupt neurotransmitter (brain chemicals) activity, while parts of the brain structure may actually shrink in response to anorexia. Unsettled eating behavior may also mean that the brain does not get the nutrients it needs, particularly concerning during adolescence when the brain is still developing.

Anosognosia is a term used in neurology to refer to a lack of an aware-ness of a deficit due to brain damage. For example, sometimes after a stroke, the person is completely unaware of having both a right and a left side of the body, and may only perceive or tend to one side.

Anosognosia is not the same as denial. A person with denial must be capable of thinking clearly enough to use denial as a defense mech-anism. In anosognosia, the malnutrition has damaged the brain to the point where the individual is not capable of processing denial as a defense mechanism.[9]

Eating disorders can certainly have an element of denial, but, while there may be psychological issues in some cases, this denial could actually be anosognosia, especially in people with anorexia, and is one of the reasons why anorexia is often so hard to treat. Indeed, according to the DSM-V, anosognosia is a defining feature of the disorder. Clinical psychologist and eating disorders expert Dr Laura Muhlheim (2020), warns against being taken in by appearances here, in that disinterest does not necessarily equal defiance. She describes how a person's refusal to believe they have an eating disorder, or to show interest in recovery, does not necessarily mean they are being willful, rebellious or resistant—it is more likely that they are simply incapable of insight.[10] Ultimately, this means those affected are less likely to seek out treatment or to participate in treatment, potentially leading to severe medical consequences. Fortunately, with renourish-ment and weight restoration, motivation and insight do come back, meaning that the individual will be more likely to engage in treat-ment or at least to realize that there is a problem.

I believe it is critical to understand this part of the illness. I have had multiple providers (healthcare, therapy, dieticians, psychiatrists, and even eating disorder specialists) tell me that I am not trying hard enough, that I am resistant and/or defiant, not progressing fast enough, non-compliant, and that I am trying to be difficult. I have even had eating disorder providers tell me I will never get better. It is extremely disheartening to hear those words over and over again from the people who are supposed to be helping you. It is not motivating at all, and in my opinion, hinders the entire recovery process. In addition, it is frustrating to put all your effort into treatment, even when you do not believe in the problem or in the severity of the issue, only to be told that you aren't good enough. It reenforces the belief that "I will never be good enough anyways, so why should I bother to try?"

I have had anorexia for almost two decades. I do have insight that I have a disorder; however, most of the time I lack the awareness about its severity. When I was in the ICU for a month because of my eating disorder, I felt guilty that I was taking away a bed from another individual who actually needed help and had a problem more severe than I.

The brain is powerful, treat it as such.

HOW EATING DISORDERS AFFECT YOUR BODY

I'll tell you a secret. No part of the body goes unaffected!

Eating Disorders
How They Affect the Body

Brain:
depression, low self-esteem, brain fog, dizziness, anxiety, fear of weight gain, memory loss

Kidneys:
kideny stones, kidney failure, injuries related to diuretic abuse decrease kidney function

Body Fluids:
dehydration, electrolyte imbalances (potassium, magnesium, sodium), anemia

Intestines and Stomach:
constipation, bloating, diarrhea, poor digestion

Skin:
bruise easily, dry skin, brittle nails and hair, yellow skin, abrasions to knuckles (Russle's Sign)

Mouth, Throat, Cheeks, and Esophagus :
swollen cheeks, cavities, gum disease, tooth erosion, sore/irritated hroat, esophageal tear or rupture

Cardiovascular:
low pulse, low blood pressure, heart rhythm abnormalities, weakening and shrinking of heart, heart failure

Hormones:
irregular/absent period, infertility, underactive thyroid, decreased immunity

Muscles, Joints, and Bones:
weakness, loss of muscle, bone loss, fatigue, swollen joints, aches and pains

RE-FEEDING AND ITS COMPLICATIONS

It is time to get a little science-y and nerdy. I have interacted with many health care providers and physicians who were unaware of some of the most dangerous complications on re-feeding a patient with an eating disorder. Patients and support members should also be aware of these complications.

What is re-feeding? Re-feeding is when you re-introduce nourishment into the body after a period of severely restricted eating. This is a natural if delicate process which, if properly handled, should do no harm. Re-feeding syndrome, however, is a dangerous, potentially fatal condition that can occur when re-feeding is carried out too quickly, and is caused by shifts in insulin and electrolyte levels in the body as more food is introduced. (See below.)

Even though the body is desperate for nutrition to survive, re-feeding a severely malnourished person can lead to extreme and deadly complications. Re-feeding has several uncomfortable effects on the individual, for example, abnormal swelling in hands and feet, severe bloating and other gastrointestinal issues, blood sugar abnormalities, fatigue, electrolyte abnormalities, and hyper-metabolism. While this book does not deal in definitions of eating disorders, or analyze their ramifications, I would like to draw your attention to a couple of serious complications that can potentially lead to death.

- Re-feeding syndrome—This can occur if an extremely malnourished person is given food too quickly, and usually presents within the first three to five days. When the body is in a malnourished state, it heavily relies on fat and muscle for energy. Once food is introduced back into the body, the body switches back to primarily carbohydrate metabolism.[11] This leads to major shifts in fluids, electrolytes, and some hormones (insulin). Low phosphorus is the hallmark of re-feeding syndrome. Magnesium and potassium levels may also drop to critically low levels.

- Does anyone remember ATP from high school science class? ATP, or adenosine triphosphate, is the cell's main energy unit. It has many purposes, but is extremely important in metabolic processes and storing energy for the body. When someone begins to eat again, the production of ATP increases. When ATP production increases, the body must pull phosphorus from the cells to create energy, leading to low phosphorus levels, especially if the person already has depleted electrolytes. Magnesium is also part of ATP production, which is why someone's magnesium levels may decrease when eating is resumed.[12]

- Insulin is one of the hormones affected during the re-feeding process. With an increase in food, blood glucose or sugar levels rise and stimulate the body to release more insulin, causing fluid retention as water, and for phosphate, glucose, magnesium and potassium enter into the cells. Potassium levels, already low from insufficient nourishment, drop and swelling accumulates.[13] These electrolyte and fluid disturbances are what cause re-feeding syndrome.

- Re-feeding syndrome can lead to weakness, confusion, difficulty breathing, cardiac abnormalities and dysrhythmias, heart failure, seizures, coma, and death.[14]

Pseudo-Bartter syndrome is a complex mix of metabolic abnormalities seen in eating disorders. Individuals who engage in purging behaviors are at risk for developing this syndrome. It is due to the body's natural response to chronic dehydration, which causes electrolyte imbalances as mentioned above. Symptoms may last for up to three weeks and can be significantly mentally distressing for the patient.

- In Pseudo-Bartter syndrome, to compensate for the chronic dehydration, the hormone aldosterone is excreted by the adrenal glands to signal the kidneys to retain salt and water so as to maintain blood pressure stability. When someone stops purging behaviors, they may end up with severe swelling due to the body's natural response of releasing increased levels of aldosterone. During this process, potassium is lost in the urine. If a healthcare provider prescribes excessive or rapid fluid repletion, it will worsen the situation.[15]

- If potassium is not replaced, the person will end up in cardiac arrest.

- Diuretics will exacerbate the condition and worsen the low

potassium, with the exception of Aldactone (spironolac-
tone). Aldactone is considered a mild diuretic and works
differently than other diuretics. Instead of wasting potassium in the urine, it retains potassium.

- If Pseudo-Bartter Syndrome is not properly diagnosed or
treated, the excess fluid and electrolyte abnormalities can
lead to an increased workload on the heart and lungs, resulting in heart failure and respiratory distress and failure.[16]

Unfortunately, over time my body has become less resilient to the
medical effects of an eating disorder. The year 2021 was especially
difficult for me. I entered an inpatient (IP) treatment center early in
the year. When I arrived, my blood pressure was unstable, so they
placed me in a wheelchair until further notice. I slowly started the
re-feeding process as expected (I had done this a few times before),
but this time my body felt different. After a few days, my blood pressure was more unstable. I felt out of breath doing the simplest tasks,
and my body was so weak that I couldn't even hold myself up over
the sink to brush my teeth. My labs were drawn and my electrolytes,
particularly my phosphorous levels, came back critically low. I had to
be sent to the local hospital to get IV electrolyte replacement. I spent
four days in hospital and was then transferred back to the treatment
center—only for it to happen all over again.

After the second hospitalization, the treatment center told me I was
too unstable for their IP program and needed medical stabilization
before I could participate in any more treatment. My mother was
required to fly to the state I was residing in to pick me up and take
me home. Well, when I got home, all of my re-feeding problems
resolved. My body went back to a state where it was used to surviving off almost nothing because I stopped eating again.

Of course, I continued rapidly to lose more weight, to the point where treatment wasn't an option if I wanted to live. I contacted almost all of the IP (inpatient) and Res (residential) treatment centers on my insurance and was denied by every single one of them. (Inpatient is typically when you are treated at a hospital, sometimes in a home-like setting depending on the treatment center, and Res is a more domestic or home-like environment for longer term treatment alongside other individuals.) Either I was too sick for their IP/Res criteria or they required me to go to ACUTE Center for Eating Disorders to get medically stable enough before transitioning into an IP program. ACUTE, in short, is an ICU specialized in medically treating eating disorders and those severely malnourished due to other health conditions. Going to ACUTE was an issue due to my insurance. They did not pay for ACUTE's services. I had to get a waiver signed and approved from the insurance company in order to receive medical care. Fortunately, I was able to get coverage but it took a few weeks to receive it.

When finally admitted to ACUTE in Denver, I could barely walk, let alone stand for more than a few minutes. Prior to my arrival, my doctor told me my labs looked like an end-stage cancer patient. She also stated that I qualified for the diagnosis of aplastic anemia (bone marrow stops producing all vital cells) and had to get a transfusion prior to flying. ACUTE took care of my electrolyte abnormalities and severe dehydration, but were cautious and vigilant about re-feeding since I had already had the syndrome before. I was also a high-risk patient for Pseudo-Bartter Syndrome, so they started me on Aldactone to prevent and reduce significant swelling. The medical care they provided was excellent. I spent a month in ACUTE ICU and then was stable enough to transfer to another facility. Again, insurance made that difficult, so I ended up going home with a feeding tube.

From then on, it has been a cycle of entering the hospital or treatment center for abnormal labs, dehydration to the point of giving myself an acute kidney injury (aka acute renal failure), and many other issues. Over the years I have come to realize that I am not infallible. That my eating disorder really does have a chance of killing me. I'm not special. Eating disorders do not make anyone special. An eating disorder doesn't make decisions about who gets to live and who dies. It is a very important lesson I learned the hard way; however, it has given me insight and gratitude. Gratitude toward my body for what it can still do and what it has endured, and insight into my life.

4

EFFECTS
ON LIFESTYLE

The impact of an eating disorder will be different from person to person. From experience, the impact is almost never positive. All the disorder does is give you a short-term, false sense of hope, calmness, and so on—the feeling of control that you desire, so you do not have to cope with all the negative aspects of your life.

My disorder has taken too many things from me, especially time, opportunities, and money. I've lost friends. I've missed holidays, time spent with my family and my precious dog, Henry. I've had to forego relationship opportunities. I lost my job as a nurse, which in turn led to me to feel that I lost part of my identity and purpose in life. Furthermore, I had to drop out of graduate school even though I had one year left. I own a condo and had to rent it out the last three years and live with my parents. I wasn't able to take care of myself independently, so I've also lost my independence. I believe losing my sense of self and purpose has impacted me the most. It creates a feeling of hollowness or emptiness. Have you ever had that lost empty feeling about yourself?

Sometimes I throw myself a little pity-party, but for the most part, I try not to feel sorry for myself or ask, "Why me?" The things I have lost are due to my actions, unconsciously of course, but sitting around crying about it will not change the past, present or future. When you lose something, you learn. I now know what I value most and have gratitude for all that I do have. When you experience so many difficult situations, you gain a more appreciative perspective on life.

5

MOST COMMON EATING DISORDER MYTHS DEBUNKED

It's time to weed out the fake news and actually look at the evidence! Knowledge is everything.

MYTH 1–EATING DISORDERS ARE A CHOICE

Umm, before I dive into the actual facts and research, let's get this straight. Why the hell would anyone want to choose to put themselves through multiple hospital/treatment stays, destroy their body, and ruin their life? It isn't a choice. It just happens. It is no more of a choice to live with an eating disorder as it is to live with an autoimmune disorder or cancer. I will say though, the person with the eating disorder does have a choice on recovery. I hate saying it, but it is true.

Yes, eating disorders are a psychiatric disease, but they do have physiologic effects on the body, which in turn, essentially exacerbates the disease itself.

Have you heard of the Minnesota Starvation Experiment? After WW2, scientists and medical professionals wanted to learn how to re-feed the starved individuals from concentration camps without accidentally killing them in the process. Discovered during this time, re-feeding syndrome, a result of rapidly feeding the starved individuals, was ultimately their cause of death -not starvation. In this study, 36 healthy men (without any history of eating problems) were taken and fed an average diet of 3200 calories for three months. Researchers observed their eating habits, behavior, and cognition. During phase 2 of the experiment, the men's caloric intake was cut in half and they were obligated to exercise 20 miles a week, although this was split up into a few miles per day and many of the men avoided excessive activity where possible.

This unethical experiment produced shocking results. During the time the participants willingly semi-starved, it became apparent that their cognitions, behaviors, and eating habits significantly changed, especially as time went on. The participants became withdrawn, mood became labile, food or food related shows/magazines became an obsession, and at mealtimes, the men developed strange food rituals, such as cutting food into a certain size, taking hours to eat meals, licking their plates and so on.

The results of this study tell us that the more malnourished the brain becomes, the more obsessed it becomes with food, and the more prone it is to developing eating disorder traits. In essence, a person with an eating disorder who is actively in a malnourished state will perpetuate their disorder due to metabolic changes in the body.[17]

Eating disorders are considered a bio-psycho-social disease. Simply put, genetics load the gun, environment pulls the trigger. More recent studies, have discovered that eating disorders are linked to an abnormality on chromosome 12, which makes sense because eating disorders tend to run in families. According to psychologist and therapist Margot Rittenhouse (2019), genes are approximately 60% responsible for the development of anorexia nervosa.[18] More interestingly, the most intricate genome study done on anorexia, conducted by University of North Carolina (UNC) College of Medicine found that the abnormal part of chromosome 12 affected was in the same area as Type 1 Diabetes and other autoimmune disorders. The genetic studies also found that anorexia nervosa is strongly correlated with neuroticism and schizophrenia, indicating that it indeed is a psychiatric illness.[19] The association with insulin metabolism and other autoimmune disorders does indicate that there is potentially a metabolic component to the illness as well. These findings are relatively new in the scientific world and do need more exploring.

MYTH 2—YOU HAVE TO LOOK A CERTAIN WAY TO HAVE AN EATING DISORDER

Besides myth number one, this myth is probably the most incorrect, frustrating and irritating myth out there! I know I am not alone in this thought. Eating disorders come in ALL shapes and sizes and your shape or size is NOT the only determining factor of the severity of your illness. I cannot emphasize this enough. Eating disorders DO NOT HAVE A LOOK. You cannot look at someone and know for sure if someone has a disorder. If there is only one thing you take away from this book, I hope that it is having this myth debunked.

Yes, frequently people with restrictive disorders do tend to be smaller in size, but that is not always the case. In fact, most people with eating disorders are at a normal weight or may even be above average weight, even when they primarily have restrictive behaviors.[20] Society has set a false and detrimental belief that to have an eating disorder you have to look a certain way, eg very skinny or emaciated. In fact, the National Association of Anorexia and Associated Eating Disorders (ANAD) states that less than six percent of people with an eating disorder are diagnosed as being underweight.[21]

Focusing on how someone looks can be extremely damaging for the person. By telling them that they do not "look" like they have a problem, they may feel too embarrassed or ashamed to get the help that they really need. In essence, it exacerbates the problem. The person may think, "I'm too fat to get help," or, "It's not that bad because I'm not extremely underweight," or, "I'm not sick enough or good enough at my disorder." This causes them to continue or even to exacerbate eating disorder behaviors.

I have been in treatment with people of all shapes and sizes. Another important point to note is that weight does not determine the severity of the disorder (screw the DSM severity scales, as I mentioned earlier, it's all for insurance!) Since I have been in treatment multiple times, my weight has fluctuated, sometimes significantly over time. I can say that my eating disorder was just as bad, if not worse at my highest adult weight (mentally) than at my lowest adult weight. Also, as I have gotten older, my body has become less resilient to the malnutrition and becomes more unstable at higher weights than it used to when I was younger. I might look normal on the outside but I can tell you my blood work, brain, bones, and my organs are not healthy on the inside!

MYTH 3—EATING DISORDERS ARE NOT THAT SERIOUS

Whenever I hear this, my eyes literally roll into the back of my head and my brain starts fuming about how uneducated society is about eating disorders. To make matters worse, it is not even their fault. Mental health stigma, lack of education in schools and health care professions, and the media contribute to lack of understanding.

In addition, there is a serious lack of funding on eating disorder research in comparison to other mental health issues. In 2017, *World Psychiatry* published an article about the lack of funding in the eating disorder realm. According to this article, in the U.S., eating disorders receive approximately $0.73 per affected individual. In contrast funding for schizophrenia is $86.97 per affected individual.[22] Although I am grateful for the money used in research, it is disappointing to see how much less the funding is in comparison to other mental illnesses. In March 2022, the Department of Health and Human Services (HHS)—through the Substance Abuse and Mental Health Services Administration (SAMHSA) announced that $35 million would be granted to strengthen mental health support in children and young adults.[23] Of course, each one of these mental illnesses deserve to receive that amount of money in funding for research and grants. It does, however, leave me questioning why the funding is so little in comparison, especially when it has the highest mortality rate of any psychiatric illness.[24] Furthermore, 97% of sufferers report significant impairment in function that can be equated to schizophrenia and autism.[25] Since it is common for people with eating disorders to suffer from co-morbid depression or substance abuse, it would make sense to increase the funding. It makes me wonder if it is due to the stigma against eating disorders.

According to ANAD, eating disorders are among the deadliest mental illnesses, only second to opioid overdose.[26] The National Eating Disorders Association (NEDA) states that up to 20 percent of individuals with chronic anorexia will die, and up to half of those deaths are related to suicide.[27] Which means that eating disorder prevention is also suicide prevention. Furthermore, community studies show that the mortality rates for other types of eating disorders have similar mortality rates to anorexia. I don't know about you, but as a nurse, a 20 percent mortality rate doesn't sound very good. One death is too many in my opinion.

Plain and simple, eating disorders kill. I tell you now, I have had friends die from this disorder, and seen other friends end up in multi-organ failure and needing transplants, due to this disease. It's painful to experience and extremely painful to watch my friends suffer.

MYTH 4—EATING DISORDERS ARE ALL ABOUT FOOD:

Well, yes and no. They actually aren't about food. Say what? Eating disorders *present* in a way that focuses on food, weight, shape, compulsive exercise, and other "odd" behaviors around/related to food. These are all symptoms of an underlying unresolved issue. In fact, some eating disorders, like ARFID (avoidant restrictive food intake disorder, see 1, What is an eating disorder, above) do not even concern weight or shape. Despite eating disorders and addictions being different in nature, regarding behaviors, I view them as very similar disorders. Why? Because generally speaking, they all share a root cause. The difference is how the individual deals with their core issues and the fact that addicts can abstain from their drug, whereas people with eating disorders must eat to survive. Most treatment programs (eating disorder or addiction) have tracks for dual-diagnosis or co-occurring disorders. Again, it is because they all stem from a core issue that needs resolving. *The International Journal of Eating Disorders* has documented that at least half of the people suffering from and eating disorder also suffer from a drug or alcohol abuse problem. Furthermore, approximately

35% of people with substance use disorders also have a co-occurring eating disorder. People with bulimia are more likely to have a substance use disorder compared to restrictive disorders (AN, ARFID)[28]

Since the eating disorder/substance use disorder come from a distressing root cause, it means that their maladaptive behaviors are serving a function and even a kind of coping mechanism. Here are some examples of functions they can serve:

- To feel in control

- Emotion regulation (to fill a void, feel comfort, to numb out, control anger)

- To deal with a traumatic experience/s

- Provides an identity and is predictable in nature

- Avoidance of intimacy

- For feelings of safety or protection (may want a smaller body or want to gain weight to look less attractive and therefore feel less vulnerable to predators. This is also in line with trauma)

- To deal with bullying

- To fit into societal standards of certain sports

MYTH 5—EATING DISORDERS ARE A YOUNG, WHITE, RICH WOMAN'S DISEASE

Picky as people with eating disorders may be, eating disorders aren't fussy. People of all ages, genders, ethnicities, cultures, or social class are affected by an eating disorder. Repeat that previous sentence.

National Eating Disorders Association (NEDA) states that even though gay, bisexual, and transgender males are more likely to develop an eating disorder than straight males, the vast majority of male eating disorder sufferers are heterosexual.

Also, according to NEDA, one in three people who have an eating disorder are male,[29] although this number may not be completely accurate due to different reasons, for example:

- The prevalence of eating disorders in males is probably higher than shown by statistics due to cultural bias. It is stigmatized as a female disorder or a gay male problem. Because of these biases, men are less likely to seek treatment.

- Men also sometimes present slightly different in their behaviors, making it more difficult to diagnose. For example, some males try to reach an unattainable muscular body type by compulsively exercising to gain muscle, and resort to disordered eating in efforts to further attain their goal.

As regards to age, eating disorders are primarily diagnosed during teenage years; however, eating disorders are seen in the middle adult to older adult range, too. I personally have been in treatment with women in their 60s and 70s. Typically, when eating disorders are seen in the "older" population or basically anyone in their late 20s or older, (I am 31 and considered old for an eating disorder!) the person has suffered from a persistently chronic disorder, or did achieve a period of remission (long or short) and have relapsed into their disordered behaviors.[30]

MYTH 6–EATING DISORDERS ARE ABOUT VANITY AND ARE USED AS A WAY TO GET ATTENTION. PEOPLE CAN JUST "SNAP OUT OF IT" OR BE "ANOREXIC FOR A WEEK"

I want to smack someone when I hear comments like those. Is that mean? Maybe it will knock some sense into them. I hate to break it to you, but eating disorders do not work like that. You cannot be anorexic for a week. Eating disorders are more of an issue with compulsion (think OCD, or obsessive compulsive disorder) than an issue with self-control. The eating disorder brain becomes more and more irrational over time, eventually leading to uncontrollable urges to engage in a compulsion/behavior and perform rituals to reduce anxiety (or other distressing emotion).[31]

Eating disorders cannot be snapped out of, nor can people "pull themselves together" and simply put aside what some see as willful, attention-seeking behavior. As mentioned before, eating disorders are a complex psychiatric illness with bio-psycho-social components that almost always requires some professional help. Generally, the professional help includes a team consisting of a psychiatrist, a psychologist or therapist, and a registered dietician who preferably specializes in eating disorders. (It really makes a difference when they are specialized). Supportive friends and/or family are always a bonus!

Depending on the severity, length of illness, and patient motivation to engage in recovery, not all people with eating disorders will need to go to a treatment center. People may start at a lower level of care (LOC). No matter what LOC you need, you will always be "sick enough" to need and deserve help. Don't let you brain or anyone else trick you into thinking otherwise.

I think there is a bit of confusion here, caused by our society's emphasis on being thin as a desirable vanity measure. So, to summarize:

- Short-term diets to lose weight for a social function or just as way to lose weight quickly = fad diet/ disordered eating and are generally socially acceptable.

- Long-term starvation, bingeing and purging, and excessive exercise despite the cost of health and wellness, which need professional help to stop behaviors = eating disorder.

MYTH 7—TREATMENT WILL CURE AN EATING DISORDER

If only it were that easy! If it were, nobody would ever relapse, and treatment centers would start to go out of business or wouldn't even exist. Treatment for any eating disorder is a process. For some, it can take several years to achieve a state of recovery. The turtle wins the race in this process. Being in IP or Res treatment sucks (that's an understatement). I can vouch for that. To be honest, though, being in IP or Res is actually supposed to be the easier part of recovery. You are in an environment with 24/7 care and support. You live in a bubble, away from events or triggers that have contributed to or exacerbated your illness and you are surrounded by other people who "get it".

Recovery is not about doing it right, it's more about how you treat yourself when you are struggling. The concept of forgiving yourself for slipping and practicing an act of self-care instead of berating yourself can make a huge difference in whether you continue to move forward towards recovery, or spiral back into old behaviors and a full-blown eating disorder.

Most if not all treatment programs follow a step-down protocol, whereby treatment is tailored off gradually according to individual progress. This means that once a person has shown their treatment team that they are ready for a lower LOC, they will step down to partial hospitalization (PHP), and then to intensive outpatient (IOP). After IOP, they graduate treatment and work with their home treatment team for ongoing maintenance.

Every step-down in LOC exposes the person to more triggers, puts them under more accountability, and involves less support. The transition can be difficult at first and is an expectation.

Just as in addictions and other mental illness, such as depression, every person with an eating disorder is prone to a slip, lapse, or relapse, especially during a time of stress. Relapse rates are high and expected in the recovery process. Relapsing does not mean you are a failure. It is an opportunity to learn, and to find what you need so you can cope with the current or new issue in a healthier manner.

6

MEDICAL TRAUMA

"A note to anyone who needs to hear it: We don't 'get over' or 'move on' from our trauma. We are forced to make space for it. We carry it. We learn to live with it. And, sometimes we thrive in spite of it"

UNKNOWN

From personal experience and research, psychological and medical trauma are very common among people with eating disorders. Either the traumatic event triggered the eating disorder, or the individual already had a trauma and is accumulating medical trauma from their eating disorder, or medical trauma exacerbates all the above. Since trauma and post-traumatic stress disorder (PTSD) are common among individuals with eating disorders, especially those with purging behaviors, most treatment facilities offer a dual diagnosis program, trauma track, or trauma treatment services, such as eye movement desensitization and reprocessing (EMDR). Eating disorders are a way to cope and feel in control of life situations and the emotions that go along with them; unfortunately, many individuals end up using an eating disorder to cope with their trauma. To those individuals, the eating disorder is helpful in the moment, but in the long term, it actually prevents them from coping and being in control.

49

So, what is trauma? The American Psychological Association (APA) defines it as an emotional repose to a terrible event. To dig deeper, the DSM-V defines trauma as an "exposure to actual or threatened death, serious injury, or sexual violation". Exposure is further defined as "directly experiencing the traumatic event, witnessing the event, learning of a trauma happening to a close family member or friend, or being repeatedly exposed to aversive details about a traumatic event".[32] Trauma is subjective—what one person may experience as a traumatic event, another may not. A person's coping skills, social support, history of past mental health conditions, past experiences, beliefs, distress tolerance, and level of resilience determine whether or not an event is going to overwhelm a person's nervous system and incite a trauma response.

There are different types of traumas, distinguished by being a big "T" or a small/little "t". Big "T" fits the DSM-V definition of trauma, where life or body integrity may be threatened. Typically, a big "T" event is more likely to lead to PTSD. Examples include war, abuse, terrorism, and natural disasters. Little "t" events are described as ego-threatening, producing feelings of helplessness. An accumulation of little "t" or less pronounced events, can still cause as much damage and malfunctioning as a big "T" experience. Examples of little "t" happenings might include divorce, infidelity, bullying, and legal issues. Unfortunately, in my opinion, the "lesser pronounced" events are easily dismissed, downgraded, or overlooked by family, caregivers, or even professionals.[33]

So, where does medical trauma fall under? Technically it could be a big "T" or little "t" depending on the event, for example, getting run over by a car versus having an invasive procedure done.

Medical trauma refers to a person's psychological and physiological response to a negative experience in health care. Experiences may include pain, invasive procedures, birth trauma, cancer, or receiving dismissive or poor treatment by providers.[34] This type of trauma can look similar to or meet the requirements for a PTSD diagnosis. Some of these symptoms include avoidance of doctors or hospitals, hypervigilance, intrusive thoughts/memories or nightmares, sleep disturbances, flash backs, and depression/anxiety. Medical trauma does not just affect the person with the negative experience. Family, loved ones, and care-takers are affected too.

Medical Trauma = f(Patient × Diagnosis)

(Procedures × Medical Staff × Medical Environment)[35]

Before I get into ways to cope, I will share some of my own experiences of medical trauma (nursing related and personal) to help create a clear picture of everything you just read.

When I worked as a nurse in the ER, I witnessed many traumatic events happen to people, and have also become traumatized by what I have seen. I believe it ultimately led me to suffer from vicarious trauma and compassion fatigue. I still clearly remember the suicidal patient who came in for a gunshot wound to the head and the suicidal young woman who hung herself. She had very pronounced ligature marks on her neck.

The man who was in a car accident, where his car burst into flames, still sits in my mind every day. With the exception of his face and his torso, his entire body burned to the bone. I witnessed an esophageal rupture in a cancer patient, that led to massive amounts of blood forcefully spewing out of him to the point that he was choking on his own blood. The amount of blood everywhere was horrifying, but it was more painful watching the patient suffer. The terror in his eyes left a mark.

I will never forget the day where the wife of her husband came up to me, gave me a hug, and begged me to not let her husband die. I didn't know what to say to her other than "I will try my best" even though I knew the odds were extremely slim (aortic dissection). We moved him into our trauma bay and continued CPR, all while the wife stood there and watched her husband die. When the doctor called the time of death, all I could do was quietly say, "I'm sorry" to the lady. Witnessing people obtain major physical injuries is difficult and stressful, but seeing the reactions of family members is almost worse. I know what grief feels like. The patient is no longer suffering—the family now holds the suffering.

In addition to everything I have witnessed, I have been verbally and physically abused by many of the patients I took care of. I've been bitten, scratched, kicked in the abdomen and punched. I have been called every degrading name in the book. I have had full, used urinals thrown towards my head. Worst of all, I have been sexually harassed by a number of male patients. Patients have taken opportunities to touch parts of my body that I had not given them consent to touch. Unfortunately, talking to the charge nurse or asking for a reassignment does not actually do that much to help the situation unless there is a male nurse willing to trade a patient. You are stuck with what you get. I understand that patients are not at their best when they come into the ER, but I have enough self-worth to know that it is not okay to treat anyone like that, let alone the person they came to get help from. Nursing has changed significantly in my eight years of work. Honestly, it makes me sad, and I wish I could make it change. The system has been broken for a long time, and the Covid-19 pandemic started to expose to the public how broken the system really is. Despite all the challenges I faced as a nurse, I would do it all over again, because I have this inherent need to care for others, even if it causes me suffering.

Apart from my experiences as a medical professional, I have endured many instances of medical trauma. Multiple times I have admitted to the hospital or ER for electrolyte abnormalities, severe dehydration, acute kidney failure, cardiac abnormalities and more. Every time I have to go to the hospital, the doctors straight up tell me that they don't know how treat eating disorders, or completely dismiss the reasons why I am there. In their defense, they do not get much training on the subject of eating disorders. It is frustrating, because I have to tell the medical staff to check certain labs and to avoid certain medications so that I will not end up in heart failure. I have even gotten comments about not being thin enough or looking sick enough to have a problem. Some health care workers think it's funny and harass me about my weight, or repeatedly ask me what my weight is, or try to get me step on the scale even though they know I go in with specific instructions for this to not happen.

Many times, the doctor will send me to the psychiatric ward because they feel I am a liability even though I had no intentions of hurting myself or others. The psych ward is more psychologically detrimental to me (and possibly to others) than it is helpful. I would go days without eating, get re-traumatized by other patients' behavior (including constant sexual harassment by the male patients. Telling the staff made no difference.) I would hide in my room, and then when something physically/medically happened to me, they would blame it on me and say I was purposely being dramatic and attention-seeking. Can't win! I am just a crazy person to all staff members. The worst is that they play the "nurse card" on me. They tell me I know better and, therefore, should automatically do better because I have the medical knowledge. If only! Wouldn't I be saving myself a lot of trouble? But mental disorders are not logical. You cannot force an illogical disorder suddenly to see things logically.

Eating disorder treatment centers are never fun. Many times, I have been administratively discharged from treatment for being "noncompliant or not trying hard enough, or progressing too slowly, or because they can't help me". First of all, that makes me feel like more of a failure, reinforces all the negative beliefs I have about myself and kills any hope that I had. Honestly, it is hurtful to face so many rejections.

You begin to wonder if it is even worth trying (it is, don't lose hope!). Before I was accepted into a treatment center at an IP level, I had to spend a month at a specialized ICU unit for eating disorders. Their medical care was fantastic, but it does take a toll mentally. My nasogastric tubes (NGTs), also known as feeding tubes, kept exploding on me and despite being flushed with specific enzymes to prevent this, my tube would continue to clog and had to be replaced almost every few days... sometimes at 2am. At one treatment center, I consider I experienced borderline patient abuse. I have had many NGTs inserted before, and yes inserting them is uncomfortable always. This center attempted to place an NGT in and was unsuccessful multiple times. I told the nurse that it was extremely painful and asked her to stop. Instead, she got an extra nurse who held me down and restrained me against my will while the original nurse forced a tube up my nose. My nose was gushing blood all down my shirt while I screamed during the whole procedure. The nurse yelled at me and asked why I was being difficult and behaving poorly. When they finally got the tube inserted, they shoved me out to the hallway in my wheelchair (I was wheelchair bound due to medical issues) and just let me sit there and sob. Not a single staff member came up to me for support.

Unfortunately, things got worse, even though I was accepting my tube feeds and working on increasing my food intake. They decided that I would be better off in a secluded room without a roommate and any of my possessions. Therapy was withheld from me and I was not allowed to attend groups. They operated via punishment, not with encouragement and positive reinforcement. This did not make any sense to me, but the laws of that state make it very easy to certify (mental hold) mental health patients for extended periods of time. Most of the patients there were already certified and I was absolutely terrified of that happening to me, so I never asked to leave. Luckily, my mother was able to help me get out of there.

Recently, I went to a detox center because I thought it was the right thing to do. Turns out that it was the worst decision I made in a long time. I was taking excessively high doses of Xanax (a short-acting and very addictive benzodiazepine). Prior to admission, the detox center told me that I would do a taper with another longer acting benzodiazepine. Doing so, would prevent me from having a seizure or become delirious and potentially die (alcohol and benzos are the most dangerous to withdrawal from), but instead they refused to give me taper medication and cut me cold turkey. Even when my blood pressure met all the parameters, I was not given medication. This is medically dangerous and can lead to long-term effects known as post-acute withdrawal syndrome (PAWS) or even death. I was only allowed Vistaril (basically Benadryl) and an anti-seizure medication.

The eight days of detox were the most painful and frustrating days of my life. I turned into a person full of a rage that I didn't think I was even capable of. Detox is no joke. I left against medical advice and contacted my own psychiatrist to do a taper at home. After almost a month, despite being on taper medication, I was still having several concerning withdrawal effects. I was abusing my prescribed medication; however, I believe it was due to my uncontrolled anxiety and having a physical tolerance to the medication. In any event, I desperately needed help that I simply wasn't getting.

It's fair to say that all of the trauma and medical trauma has worsened my condition. It is almost like a cycle of self-destruction. I endure a medical or mental trauma, I have a hard time coping with it and want to feel in control of my situation, so I engage in eating disorder behaviors that eventually lead back to the beginning of the cycle…

COPING TIPS

If you find yourself dealing with any sort of trauma, there are several coping skills you can use to decrease your distress.

- First, I want you to know that none of it is your fault and feeling the way you do is not a sign of weakness.

- Second, I want you to recognize that your trauma is real and worthy of acknowledgment, validation, and treatment, regardless of the severity.

- Third, know that you are not being melodramatic. If anything, you are probably downplaying or rationalizing the event subconsciously to protect yourself. It is an act of avoidance and common among traumatized individuals. You are not alone.

Ways to cope:[36]

- Mindfulness or deep breathing exercises.

- Socialize, even if you don't want to. Isolation will make things worse.

- Talk to a psychiatrist about medications if necessary.

- Attend trauma support groups. Support is key!!!

- Therapy/counseling.

- Advocate for yourself. It isn't selfish, I promise.

Therapies that are evidenced based:

- Trauma focused therapy, preferably with a trauma specialist.

- Eye movement desensitization and reprocessing (EMDR).

- Cognitive behavioral therapy (CBT).

- Cognitive processing therapy (CPT).

- Prolonged exposure therapy.

WOUNDS HEAL BY DEGREES

"What wound did ever heal but by degrees?"

WILLIAM SHAKESPEARE (OTHELLO)

I've got wounds; some are old and some are new.

*Some are minor scrapes of the skin; others are more like
a stab to my heart or a fracture to my soul.*

*I see the superficial ones heal quickly, mostly without intervention,
although some need a few stitches to help repair.*

Do not be fooled, for wounds are not always visible to the naked eye.

*I also have wounds full of despair. They ferociously fester underneath
the seemingly normal outward appearance and ooze within
my body causing more hurt, shame, anger and sadness.*

*Since these wounds are so deep, I cannot always see or feel
the tiny changes of new growth and healing.*

*We all want our wounds to heal quickly without complication, but
Shakespeare was right, "What wound did ever heal but by degrees?" To
truly grow and heal from the inside out, to build resilience, strength,
and courage, one must have patience and self-compassion and let
each wound heal degree by degree, each in their own time.*

JML

PART TWO

Rebirth and Growth

THE PHOENIX

In the last 500 years,
I have roamed the earth,
Endured through every struggle to accomplish my mission.
I have healed those in need
And given hope to those who were lost.

For I have symbolized undying perseverance
To those ready to give up,
And have allowed deep discoveries surface to their minds
So they can rebuild and renew.

But I am tired now;
I have reached the final phase of my eternal life cycle.
It is time for my destruction.

I fly to my nest,
Where my body bursts into flames
Until all that is left is a pile of ashes.
Do not fear,
For every time I burst into flames,
I will always rise from the ashes as a better version of myself.

The cycle of destruction, rebirth, transformation, and destruction
Is meant to show all the people in this world
That it is possible to rise from their own destruction and ashes,
To transform and become the version of the person they were meant to be.

JML

7

EMPATHY, COMPASSION, AND SELF-COMPASSION

Have you ever paused for a moment to think about what someone's life is like when that person has cancer, diabetes, chronic heart disease, an eating disorder or any mental illness? Sure, you can imagine that it is painful, frustrating, and/or exhausting, but have you truly stepped into their shoes and tried to live their experience for just a moment? Personally, I believe that people find it easier to be empathetic towards those suffering from medical diseases or diseases that are more outwardly noticeable than those with a mental illness. It's not just me, either—extensive research has shown that mental illness bears a noticeable stigma in our society. Even though I have suffered from both physical and mental ailments, I too, used to have a harder time being more empathetic towards those suffering from mental illness. I think it is because I did not want to face the reality of my own issues. Hello, denial!

From my nursing experience, I now have had a lot of practice stepping into my patient's shoes. I experience a glimpse of their suffering, whether it's from a minor injury or a chronic illness. I see some patients come through the emergency room (ER) time and time again. It is like we have a revolving door just for them (they should get some sort of "sky or ER miles" for their visits to help pay for their medical bills). With these patients, I can see over time that they are becoming worn out, both physically and mentally. Having a chronic illness can be very taxing on the psyche and lead to depression, and frankly, it is hard to watch this process, especially if you are empathetic.

One of the reasons I chose to work as an ER nurse was because I thought that I would not become attached to my patients. In reality, I misconstrued myself. I just wanted to spend a few hours with each patient, fix them and send them home, or stabilize them and send them to another unit. I thought that if I only spent short periods of time with people, I would not get to know them and immerse myself into their own pain and suffering. Being an empath is a blessing and a curse.

I was, and still am capable of providing empathetic and compassionate care towards patients. Selfishly, however, I did not want to feel their pain. I did not want to open myself up to the reality of their situation because I knew how it felt to be in my own suffering. Sounds contradictory, doesn't it? How can you provide empathy and compassion when you don't want to feel anything at all?

It turns out that in any case, my plan backfired, to provide empathetic and compassionate care without any of my own emotions becoming involved. It wore me down; I failed to take care of my own needs because I focused too much on those of others. I started to experience burnout from my job. It is hard to be around constant suffering, especially when you are suffering yourself.

My work as a nurse has taught me a priceless lesson. Self-compassion. I wrote about my nursing experience because it shows how neglecting self-compassion affects mental illness, mental-wellness, and recovery from and eating disorder. I thought I could keep giving from an empty cup, until my empty cup broke. You might be able to give from an empty cup for a little while, but eventually your cup will break, too, unless you start to fill it back up with self-compassion.

March 3, 2022:

Compassion. I always saw the term as something positive, like being empathetic and giving someone hope. I was taught to be a compassionate person when growing up, and in nursing school I was taught to provide compassionate care. Now, to be honest, I am not really sure what I thought the term meant until group yesterday, when the therapist leading us pointed out that it means to suffer with or for someone else. Does having a career where you are compassionate all of the time change the way I am compassionate toward myself? I guess that is where compassion fatigue comes into play. The confusing thing to me is, how can you be compassionate towards yourself if it means to suffer with yourself?—JML

I must care for myself before I can care for others. Such a simple concept, yet so difficult for me to comprehend and execute. I got a 4.0 GPA (grade point average—4 is generally regarded as the gold standard) in graduate school, yet I can't figure out how compassion equals suffering. That group really got the gears turning in my brain (if anyone smelled any smoke, that was probably my brain at work!) So, I did some research and discovered several interesting snippets of information and why empathy, compassion, and especially self-compassion are so important in our mental well-being and recovery process. The therapist was not wrong. The Latin root for compassion is *pati-* or to suffer, and the prefix *com* means with, stemming from the Latin *cum*.[37] It worked its way into the language via old French *compassion* (14th century.) When you break the word down, it literally means "to suffer with".

EMPATHY VS COMPASSION

Empathy and compassion are commonly used interchangeably; however, they are not the same. To have empathy means to have an awareness of and understanding of someone else's emotions, feelings, attitudes, and perspectives about a situation.[38] Essentially, empathy means to walk in another's shoes. Empathy usually precedes compassion, but you can be empathetic and not compassionate.

Compassion requires empathy. It is the *action* you desire to implement in order to alleviate the suffering for the person with whom you are empathizing. In short, empathy is a feeling and compassion is an action. Just like almost every action, choice, or thought, empathy and compassion have their own set of pros and cons.

Empathy

- Pros—allows us to make connections and create healthy personal relationships.

- Cons—empathizing too much can cause you to ignore or mis-identify your own emotions.

Compassion

- Pros—many studies have shown that compassion decreases depression and stress, increases self-esteem, and helps others.

- Cons—too much compassion (aka pouring from an empty cup too long) can lead to compassion fatigue, negative health complications, increase anxiety and depression, and lead to negative coping skills. If overdone, it can inhibit growth and increase personal suffering

SELF-COMPASSION

Let me ask you a question. Does a starving child or a suffering war veteran deserve compassion? Okay, now answer this question, do I deserve self-compassion? If you answered "No" for the second question, go back to the first one and start over. Yes. Everyone deserves self-compassion. So, what is self- compassion? The acclaimed clinical psychologist Dr Andreas Comninos defines self-compassion as attending to your own suffering while maintaining the intention to help others—in other words, we understand that we are suffering, and we do what we can, paying attention to our own needs.[39] One thing I do know, is that it is much easier to provide compassion toward someone other than yourself!

The great Dr Kristen Neff, a professor in educational psychology at the University of Texas, Austin, does an excellent job explaining the three elements of self-compassion and what self-compassion is not. First, Dr Kristen Neff explains that self-compassion is taking the compassion you would direct towards others, but instead, direct it toward your own suffering. It means to treat yourself with kindness, forgiveness and patience. This also means being judgment free towards self and practicing mindfulness as a way of generating goodwill and kindness toward yourself as well as others. She also makes it very clear that self-compassion is not self-pity, self-indulgence or self-esteem, nor is it a sign of weakness.[40] Providing compassion towards yourself is an individual experience.

Since I have spent a great deal of time delving into the meaning of empathy, compassion, and self-compassion, you are probably wondering, why is it so important? How will this help me in my journey to recovery from an eating disorder or other mental illness?

THE IMPORTANCE OF SELF-COMPASSION IN LIFE AND IN RECOVERY[41]

1. It is one of the most powerful resources of learning to cope and to build resilience.

2. It activates the soothing system of the brain by turning off threat signals.

3. This allows you to work through and challenge difficult feelings and experiences and grow the healthier side of yourself.

4. It is the antidote to the "inner- critic".

5. It boosts self-esteem, emotional and mental well-being (fewer negative emotions overall and fewer depression symptoms), increases resilience, and enables more compassion to be shown towards others.

6. Studies have shown that it decreases feelings of shame, eating disorder pathology, and those who practice self-compassion tend to respond more favorably to eating disorder treatment.

7. Last but not least, support systems need to maintain self-compassion during their supportive process in order to continue to help their loved one without end up with compassion fatigue. Keep your cup full!

8

VULNERABILITY, THE TWO SIDES

Whenever I used to hear the word "vulnerability" I used to cringe, slip a little eye roll in there, and think, "Ugh, not that word again! Nobody wants to be vulnerable. Vulnerability equals danger and increases my risk of being unsafe." I used to be narrow minded and to look at vulnerability only as a weakness, but over time I have broadened my beliefs, and now see vulnerability as a sign of strength. Not surprising, it is a very popular word in the treatment and therapy world. During my most recent stay in treatment, the word vulnerability was yet again brought up in group. Shocking, I know. This time, instead of zoning out, I quietly sat in my unofficially officially claimed corner chair (let's be real, everybody likes to have an unofficial assigned seat!) and listened to what the people in my group had to say and what was brought up by the therapist.

Maybe the nutrition actually allowed me to focus for once? This time I could see the word from a different perspective. I have always believed that allowing myself to be vulnerable to a therapist, a friend, a family member, and so on, would ultimately result in me getting hurt, and that nothing but pain would ever come from it. I still believe this most of the time; it's my default position and practically an automatic thought. However, now I can also see the benefits of being vulnerable. It's important for me consciously to remind myself that it can lead to growth and positive outcomes in life. You can have friendships and relationships without being vulnerable, but they will never blossom to their full potential.

I have noticed over the years that every time I go into treatment, I let my guard down just a little bit with the other patients. I feel safer being vulnerable due to shared or similar experiences. It has resulted in some of the best, supportive, and deeply connected friendships I have ever had. The first person I ever allowed myself to become vulnerable with was my roommate in treatment way back in 2008. To this day, she is still my best friend, even when we haven't talked in a while, and when we do, it's like I talked to her yesterday. I am forever grateful that we both opened up to each other and went through our treatment experience together. If we didn't, then I would be missing a special person in my life.

Now, I am not saying you need to walk up to someone and tell them every horrible detail of your life story, neatly unpack one thing at a time instead of emptying the entire suitcase at once… for every one's sake. I am suggesting that letting your guard down in certain situations at the right time might actually be beneficial in the end. I do not believe that you can heal from any mental strife without being at least a little bit vulnerable. In fact, I believe it is one of the keys to recovery.

What do you think about vulnerability? After that one group at the treatment center, I decided to write my thoughts down to try and process everything. I seem to process and understand much more easily when I write. I wanted to share with you the poems I wrote, to give you a better understanding of my thought process and help you also process what it means to be vulnerable. If you find it helpful, why not take a sheet of paper or a notebook and write down your thoughts, too?

THE DARK SIDE OF VULNERABILITY

Vulnerability opens up a side not usually shown,
Almost like tearing open a big gaping black hole.
A hole known to leave you standing there scared, alone,
Open to pain, and a feeling of no sense of control.

Vulnerability eventually will surface the long-buried hurt inside,
The hurt that has been continuously stuffed down
By harming one's self in one way or another.
Drugs, alcohol, starvation, self-harm.
I do not think the type of harm matters, or does it?
It doesn't to me, does it to you?

Vulnerability is an interesting place to step into.
You do not know what path it will lead you down.
You do not know who will be there for you
Or if you will have to walk your path alone.
Walking that path alone is much worse than keeping your demons bound inside,
Or is it?

There is always a catch.
You have to be vulnerable if you want to find out if someone is
willing to join you on your journey through the beaten path.
It is a difficult choice.
How do you choose between pain
And the possibility of a different kind of pain?
Why is that something we must even consider?

Weightless

Vulnerability leaves you open for prey.
Of course, the lion is going to attack the weakest
animal of the pack—the vulnerable one.
The one who is alone and/or injured; maimed in
some capacity and the easiest catch.
The lion knows how to sneak up on its prey,
Cautious, hidden, patient, and when ready,
It pounces at just the right moment.
Guess what? So do humans.

Being vulnerable has allowed many lions to sneak upon me and pounce.
Every lion has caught me, their prey, each time weakening me
Past the point of wanting to stand up and keep running from the predator.
I just want to stay down this time, and let it finish eating
away at the little flesh I have left for it to consume.

So far, vulnerability has not shown me mercy, or love, or trust.
I only find myself in a constant state of terror
And being unable to decide if I want to live or die.
Some people tell me that vulnerability can become a good thing.
Can it? Is it?

JML

THE BRIGHT SIDE OF VULNERABILITY

When you let the dark ominous clouds
Float above your garden,
And the earth's tears fall
From a drizzle to a downpour
And allow the tear drops to land on the pretty leaves and flowers,
Soaking them until they wilt under the weight of the water,
That is vulnerability.

Vulnerability is an expression of pain
That allows beauty to grow,
Because without the vital water of the storm,
The flowers in that pretty garden will not flourish or stand tall.
They will wither and crumble,
Leaving their dried up branches and thorns to stick out,
Where the signs of death and pain will remain.

Vulnerability allows the sparkles of light
Shine through even the darkest puffs of
Anger, sadness, shame, guilt, hate, pain, humility, and loneliness
That envelope those heavy tears.
It makes room for that small ray of sunlight to expand
Until the hot, bold, and bright rays of sun cast onto that flowerless garden,
And bring the withered leaves and crumbled flowers back to life again.

Vulnerability allows room for hope,
And hope is the key to a future
You want to behold.

JML

9

MOTIVATION IN RECOVERY

Guess what, "Nothing changes if nothing changes"

MY FRIEND MINDY

M otivation is crucial for driving any type of behavior or change. Extrinsic motivation is a psychological term used to describe motivation that comes from external sources and is to avoid punishment or to earn a reward. The behavior or change is usually unpleasant to the person; however, extrinsic motivation can lead to increased intrinsic motivation, which is more self-driven, and so is useful in the short-term. For example, a person suffering from an eating disorder or addiction may enter treatment to "get family off their back", or their job has required them to do so to remain employed. In this kind of case, the person is focusing on extrinsic factors. Intrinsic motivation comes from within the person. The behavior is rewarding in itself, tends to be self-generated, and is more effective long-term.

Intrinsic motivation is imperative and necessary for lasting recovery. You can go through treatment and graduate in remission through extrinsic motivation, although it will make the process more difficult to sustain in the long-term. Sometimes extrinsic motivation is essential to start the recovery process until the person finds their intrinsic motivation for recovery (and that is okay!)

From personal experience, I must emphasize that intrinsic motivation is necessary in the long run, because extrinsic motivations will never be enough to make or to maintain goals in recovery. With every single one of my attempts at recovery, despite what was on the line (my job, my career, my house etc), I still engaged in eating disorder and addiction behaviors. The eating disorder and my addiction always seemed to have more value to me in the end. It didn't matter how much I had already lost or was going to lose.

This concept does not only apply to me. I am not a unicorn, well maybe in a past life, but not in this current time and age! I have seen this cycle repeat many times in my friends and in other patients—despite all that is on the line, they cannot quit the behaviors that are hurting them. This is a difficult concept to understand if you have not personally experienced this. Many family members, friends and coworkers have wondered how I could continue to destroy everything that was important to me for a "high" or a lower number on the scale.

As I sat in the midst of medical detox from Xanax, I finally understood why so many people, including me, continued to fall down the path of destruction despite the consequences. Of course, I didn't want to lose my job, my career, my house or my independence. Even though I watched one value after another being destroyed, I continued to self-destruct. I never had the intrinsic motivation to recover. I focused on extrinsic motivation alone, and this is probably one of the reasons why I have continued to relapse and never quite reached a state of recovery from my eating disorder.

I do believe that I have the intrinsic motivation to stay sober from benzodiazepine addiction. I entered medical detox because I no longer wanted to rely on medication to erase all my emotions and essentially to escape from life. I wanted to be in control of my life, not to be under the control of a substance that was destroying my life and threatening my nursing career. Having internal motivators has made it easier to tolerate the distress involved in treatment, and to get through it; however, as powerful as my motivation is, I realize that I cannot do this alone. For me to be successful, I had to surrender and to accept that I needed help first, then focus on my "why". Always look for your "why".

Detox was always a horrible (understatement of the year) yet humbling experience. It is still not easy, but surrendering and accepting has made a difference. Becoming sober has become less of a chore and more of something that I value. I *got* to be in treatment and to learn how to regain control of my life. It was not I *had to* be in treatment because it's the only way to work as a nurse again. Do you see the difference? The meaning of the sentence completely changes when you replace "get to" to "have to". When you "have to" do something, the decision is no longer in your hands. When you "get to" do something, it is due to your choice and it can greatly empower you.

As someone who has done extensive eating disorder treatment (of many different modalities), I never thought that the 12-step model would be of any benefit to me. I was mistaken. Do I believe that I must follow all 12 steps exactly as they are all the time to be successful? No, but I do believe that applying some of the steps to both eating disorder and addiction treatment can be helpful for many people. These concepts do not need to be exclusive to mental health treatment either, they are beneficial to all areas in life. Guess what? Nothing changes if nothing changes. A friend of mine always reminds me of that, and it is very true. If you do want your life to be different, you have to start reacting to life differently. Switch that negative "I'm broken and helpless" mentality to a more positive thought, such as, "I'm growing and healing", and you will be surprised by how differently you start reacting to life.

THE 12 STEPS

If you're in recovery, you'll doubtless be familiar with this concept, but, for those who haven't yet come across it, what are the steps and what is a 12-step program? Briefly, the 12 steps form a program of recovery specifically tailored to the needs of people with harmful addictive behaviors. The 12-step program originated in 1935 with the creation of Alcoholics Anonymous in Akron, Ohio, and later spread out to encompass other kinds of addiction and substance abuse including drugs, compulsive gambling, overeating and relationships. Since its inception, the 12-step movement has helped millions of people.

The steps themselves start with a declaration of powerlessness over whatever substance or behavior is at stake, and then progress to a decision to turn the problem over to a higher power (however that may be defined.) The rest of the steps present a program for cleaning up your psychological act, erasing past fears and unhelpful ideas, and helping others. The steps are best worked within a group context and within the extra support of a more experienced member called a sponsor. The entire process is described as three-fold path to sobriety—physical, mental and spiritual.

10

WHAT IT IS LIKE FOR ME TO LIVE WITH AN EATING DISORDER

Some people like to personify their eating disorder, such as naming it Ana, Ed, Mia, or whatever name they have decided on. Personally, I see my eating disorder as a dementor (from Harry Potter, a dark wraith or evil spirit that could generate feelings of depression and despair, and consume a human soul). It hovers in its faceless black draping robes over my shoulder at all times and slowly sucks out my life and my soul. I like to call my eating disorder "Ed" and will refer to the term "eating disorder" as "Ed" from now on.

Unless you have been in the grip of an eating disorder, it is impossible to completely understand what it is like. It is virtually impossible for me to explain my life with anorexia. I can, however, give you a glimpse of my experience via some of my journal entries, which I hope will give you a better understanding of this disease, and what it means to live with it. Most of my journal excerpts are from more recent years and treatment admissions. I specifically selected these entries because they begin to show growth and a change in my thought process. My older journal entries, especially from when I was a teen, focus mostly on "how fat I am" and are very Ed orientated. Stepping into my shoes is not a fun journey, but, for the brave, are you ready to go for a walk?

1/13/2019:

My alarm clock goes off. It's 05:10. It's way too early. I turn onto my back and run my fingers along my hip bones. Then I run my fingers along my rib cage and feel each bump. I need to make sure my ribs and hip bones didn't suddenly disappear under a huge layer of fat while I was asleep. I take my middle finger and thumb and wrap them around my upper arm. They almost touch. I am so close—if I could just lose a little bit more weight…

As I lie there, I contemplate my existence and wonder if getting up for work and pretending to function in society is worth it at all. Most days it isn't but I muster up enough strength to get up anyways. I stumble to the door and have to hold onto the wall. My legs feel weak and heavy, my heart is pounding, and my ears are ringing. I wait for it to pass and then I walk to the bathroom to step onto the scale. I think to myself, "I ate 350 calories yesterday and took some diuretics, it should be down, right? What if it isn't? Then what? Maybe I shouldn't have eaten so much. What if I am actually retaining water from dehydration from the diuretics? Should I even step on the scale? I need to know how much I weigh". My weight dropped 0.2 pounds.

That's it? How disappointing. Fat fucking failure. I need to recheck my ribs and hip bones to make sure they are still visible. I look in the mirror and pinch my fat and recheck my bones. I stare at the wounds I inflicted on my stomach the night before.

They look angry but less inflamed. You know what? Those 0.2 pounds were useless. I can't see a difference at all. In fact, I can't see the 23-pound difference at all! My last treatment totally ruined my body. I know my weight is less and my measurements are smaller so why can't I see it? I must lose more weight.

After getting dressed, I make my way into the kitchen and make some coffee. I mull over the idea of eating breakfast. "I don't want to eat. I could get away with it. But then what if I pass out at work and they take my shirt off to do an EKG and see the cuts all over my arms and my stomach? Then they'll know how crazy I am and then everyone will talk about me and I'll be super ashamed. I'll have to quit my job and have to tell my parents some ridiculous excuse as to why I can't work there anymore and then what?" Ultimately, I decide that I should eat breakfast and that it's safe to eat as long as I eat my safe food within safe portions. I'll take away lunch to make up for the calories eaten at breakfast. Finally, I pull out the oatmeal and weigh out 32 grams and add some cinnamon and hot water.

I speed along US 1 toward the highway. I've spent so much time body checking and weighing my food that I am now running late for work. My heart pounds with anxiety over eating and being late. I try not to cry and think, "Why can't I just be thin already? I hate myself. Please don't let me have to watch anyone die today. I don't want to pretend that I have a perfect life but I also don't want anyone to know how screwed in the head I really am. Why am I always sad? I have no good reason to be. Other people have real problems to cry about. You are such a fucking loser. Get over yourself already. Am I having an identity crisis? The probability seems high. I don't know who I am or what I want anymore."

Quickly, I pull into the parking lot and race through the ambulance bay entrance, all while forcing a smile on my face and holding back my tears. Crying is weak anyways. It is essential to remain strong, I'm an emergency room nurse, people count on me to be strong. I am here to care for other people, not myself.

I'm eight hours into my 12-hour shift. Everyone but me has gone on break or at least made their way over to the cafeteria to grab some food. I've drank about 4 cups of black coffee and that's it. My stomach growled at me for a little bit but as usual, I waited it out and it stopped. Nobody noticed that I didn't eat and I'm totally ok with that. I already get enough crap from my coworkers about being vegetarian even though I know they are just having some fun annoying me about it.

On my way home I feel exhausted and weak. Did I walk enough at work? Should I have made extra rounds around the hallways to burn extra calories? Maybe I sat for too long and now I have a 50-minute drive home of more sitting. While I drive, I think about what's on my allowed list for dinner, which is stupid because I almost always eat the same thing every night—a salad consisting of lettuce, baby carrots, salsa, and sometimes tofu.

After I arrive home and shower, I open and close the refrigerator at least five times. For some reason I think that the contents that lie within it will change, or that maybe I'll be okay to pick something. What if I just let myself eat something a little higher in calories and just purge after or take some laxatives to "clean myself out"? Ugh, the thought is slightly tempting but it requires some effort and I'm too lazy for that, nor do I want to be in significant pain all night. It's just easier and safer to not eat or eat very little. I open the pantry at least five times too. Nothing is safe. After pacing, opening and closing doors, and calculating in my head for close to an hour, I chose my usual salad.

It's 22:00. I allow myself to weigh out some berries to eat. I am still under my calorie limit for the day. This would not deter me from skipping my snack; however, I am afraid of setting myself up for binge mode the next day. I am afraid of myself when I get that way. It's like my brain has gone into autopilot and I am just there mindlessly shoving food into my mouth until I feel like I'm going to explode. And then just like that, I'm back to reality and left with overwhelming guilt and horror so I punish myself and rid myself of glutton.

Now it's just about midnight. I lie in bed wondering if my heart will stop beating or if I'll wake up in the morning. Neither option seems preferable. I feel my ribs and hip bones and measure my arm one last time. Okay, I think it's finally safe to go to sleep now.—JML

∽

I wrote that excerpt in my journal after reading an article about what it was like to suffer from an eating disorder. It made me curious to delve a little deeper into my daily life of working while also battling my anorexia. To make things clear, this is just part of *my* experience— every person's experience with an eating disorder is and will appear or present differently. Until I wrote that excerpt, I honestly had no idea how mind-consuming an eating disorder is. Over time, that initial eating disorder thought quickly permeates your entire mind. It invades everything until there is nothing left but the eating disorder. This transformation can happen so quickly that you do not even realize it until it is too late.

One way to recognize how much the eating disorder consumes your life is to draw two pie charts. In the first pie chart, draw inside your chart how much of each section of your normal life takes up, and how much of it is related to the eating disorder. In the second pie chart, draw what you would like to focus on in your life, and what proportion of your life you want to focus on it. Below is an example of one of the pie charts I have drawn throughout treatment.

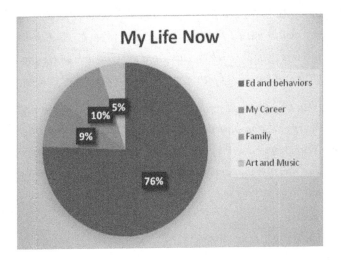

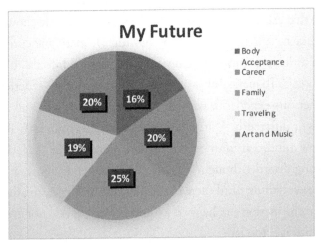

As you can see, my disorder consumes my life, crowding out normal interests and behaviors. The second pie chart was actually more difficult to construct because I did not and still do not have a clear sense of who I was, or am, without my disorder. It leaves me with the question, what kind of life do I want to live? It is a question I have been unable to answer both before going to treatment, and multiple times while in treatment. All I have to say is, well shit, that is a good question and a problematic one for me to answer. What do I want in life? I have asked myself this countless times, yet I am still never able to provide an answer.

Since I have lived the life of an Ed for almost two decades now, I do not know or remember what life is like outside of that. Is life without Ed worth it, or will it bring me more mental anguish in the end? All I know is suffering, and in a twisted way, I feel safe knowing the familiar pain of living with an Ed. Although I cannot pinpoint what I do want in life, I do know some things that I do not or no longer want in my life. I don't want to spend more time in and out of treatment or have another NGT shoved up my nose and into my stomach to be force fed. I no longer want to be a burden on anyone or cause my family more heartache, because eating disorders are a family disease. I do not want to be the problem anymore. And mostly, I no longer want to continue to be in pain.

Here, I have included several journal entries to help give you a glimpse of my thought processes and state of mind with an Ed.

6/16/21:

I have a huge mix of emotions right now. It is hard to pinpoint how I actually feel. Overwhelmed maybe? Sad? Ashamed? Disgusted? All of the above? Yesterday I made a very impulsive decision to sign out of ACUTE (basically an ICU for Ed patients and severely malnourished people) against medical advice and to fly home with a feeding tube. I just couldn't take being there any longer nor did I want to enter my third decade in the hospital. I think I was in a fight or flight mode. All of my emotions were starting to come back full force. I was having nightmares almost every single night, I could see the extent of the weight I had gained and it was all just becoming too much for me to handle.

I made the decision to leave after my team left for the day, so they would find out in the morning. Purposely I scheduled the earliest flight possible so there was no one able to certify me (90-day psychiatric hold, or retention of the patient during what is deemed to be a psychiatric emergency). I do not regret my decision to leave, but I do regret leaving without them giving me a plan, and doing it "behind their backs", so to speak. My parents didn't murder me when I arrived home but they certainly were not happy that I was home with a feeding tube.

For me, I could use this tube to my advantage or disadvantage as far as recovery goes. The pull towards weight loss is so strong right now. I almost cried when I saw my body in the mirror earlier after my shower. It has changed in so many ways and I hate the way it looks. Why does it always go to my thighs? The abdomen I can understand, the body wants to protect the vital organs, but the thighs? I want my old body back even if I felt like I was dying. Actually, I was dying. Literally dying and I still want that old body. That's so fucked up. I just don't ever see my brain being "normal" again. Hippocrates said "Let food be thy medicine and medicine be thy food", but it never makes me feel any better so how could it be thy medicine?—JML

8/3/21:

A lot has happened since I last wrote. I ended up getting Baker Acted (aka a 72hr hold, emergency commitment to a mental health treatment center if they display extreme signs of mental illness) again after telling my psychiatrist that I wanted to give up and would rather let the Ed kill me than go back to treatment. I still had the NGT in at the time. Because of the feeding tube, the hospital couldn't find placement at a psychiatric facility for me (thank God) and I ended up staying in the ER for two days. I didn't eat or drink anything during those two days and ended up passing out in the hallway walking from the bathroom. That's when the doctor decided to give me IV fluids and admit me. Not a single person offered me food or water or encouraged me to have something.

I felt so mistreated and misunderstood the whole time I was Baker Acted. It's like once you are deemed a psych patient, nobody cares about you anymore. No one checks on you, nobody tends to your needs (not all staff but a lot of them), and you are just on display for everyone to look at. You are a freak show.

After discharging from the hospital, I ended up calling another treatment center for an assessment and admission date. I admitted on 7/22/21. With my body so weak and malnourished, I almost passed out as I walked into their front door and ended up wheelchair bound for the first week. I've only been here about a week and a half and this place feels like a prison.

I live in fear of doing one thing wrong and getting certified for it. There are already several people here who are certified.

I got back from the hospital this evening. They had to send me to the hospital via ambulance for a critically low phosphorus level that needed IV replacement. I had warned them several times that my phosphorus drops to critical levels. I knew my levels were low because I felt even weaker and had a hard time breathing. The stay at the hospital wasn't too horrible, with the exception of the ER nurse who kept insisting on asking my weight, trying to guess it, and trying to get me to stand on the scale despite knowing that I came from an eating disorder treatment center. The whole process of going to the hospital, coming back to the treatment center despite not wanting to, resulted in a major panic attack.—JML

1/16/22:

I am so hungry but I am so scared to eat! I want to eat so badly but the fear of losing control or gaining weight is so overpowering. My body is failing me and I still cannot get myself to eat. My CBC (complete blood count, a blood test that tests for a wide range of disorders) looks like an end-stage cancer patient. Apparently, my bone marrow has failed to the point that I technically have aplastic anemia (where the bone marrow and stem cells do not produce enough blood cells) and severe agranulocytosis (a dangerously lowered white blood cell count) and need to get infusions to help fix it. This, plus the motivations I am trying to focus on, doesn't seem powerful enough to help me overcome this. The more malnourished I become, the higher my anxieties and fears get.

It feels like there is a lot of pressure on me to "fix" myself this time; do treatment right and leave when I am so-called cured. Obviously, that is an unrealistic expectation, but my family, my therapist, my friends, and I myself seem to be implying that expectation. This treatment center accepted me into their IP program and I will be admitting January 27th. I am absolutely terrified. I don't want my body to change. I don't want to deal with the physical or mental discomfort of re-feeding and the weight gain. Mentally, fighting has exhausted me. Why can't they just give me an NGT at home and try and recover that way. I just don't see an end to this, ever.—JML

1/24/22:

It has been a difficult day so far. It is hard to lose something (my nursing job) that you worked so hard for and put a lot of value into, and then not get the closure you were hoping for. The future will always hold new and possibly better opportunities. I will hold onto that hope and use it to motivate me to keep going when treatment/life gets hard. It's just a shame that I had to lose my job three days before going to treatment. At least I will have extra support soon enough.—JML

2/21/22:

Today is the start of NEDA week (National Eating Disorder Association) with the 2022 theme of, "See the Change, Be the Change". So many people struggle with eating disorders and are unable to get the help and care they need. I want to be part of the change. I thought just by making posts to raise awareness and sharing my story to allow people to see how it affects pretty awesome people would be enough, but then I realized that it just isn't enough. I must be the change, which is exactly what I am doing now. Choosing to go back to treatment and participate in all the ups and downs that come with it IS BEING the CHANGE. Slowly I am learning to eat more and rely less on the feeding tube, but small steps forward will lead to bigger steps forward and CHANGE. I hope my journey will inspire change in others (Ed related or something different). Eating disorders/mental illness is NOT a choice, but you can choose the outcome. -JML

From my personal experience with chronic anorexia, drug addiction, and other chronic mental health issues, I can tell you, that it is challenging to keep pushing forward. I am weary of getting my blood drawn constantly, tired of admitting in and out of the hospital for dehydration, starvation, electrolyte imbalances and other abnormal labs. Tired of getting nasogastric tubes (NGTs) shoved up my nose and into my stomach to be force feed, and most of all, exhausted fighting my own brain 24/7.

As a nurse, I especially hate being the "revolving door" or "frequent flyer" patient at the hospital and at treatment centers. The longer the illness continues, it feels like the pressure to "get better already" or "recover right this time" gets higher as time goes by. It is difficult to have that tension linger in the back of your mind while dealing with everything else. It instills a fear that you will fail yet again, and at least for me, reinforces my belief that I am a failure as a person. The list does go on. I believe it is said out of love, but it is very discouraging to hear, especially when you know how fatigued you are of fighting.

11/24/2021:

It almost seems like the older you get or the longer you have an ED, the less people give a shit about it or you and take it less seriously. It's like people are thinking, "get over it already", "she's the one doing it to herself, she shouldn't complain about anything", "she's just doing this for attention", "why can't she just eat already", "she isn't trying hard enough or just being resistant/noncompliant".

It's not that simple. I keep falling down, but I also keep getting back up because of my family and my fur-baby Henry. I didn't choose this disease, it just happened. Just like nobody decides to get cancer or diabetes. It isn't looked upon the same though (hello mental health stigma). It has broken me; taken everything from me. My body is failing me. I'm not so sure I want to get back up again. No more fighting, please. I no longer have the hopes of making a difference in people's lives, because a worthless person like me can't fix what's broken.—JML

I knew I had become tired of dealing with my chronic mental health issues, but I didn't realize how exhausted I really was until I had one last conversation with my favorite night nurse at my most recent treatment encounter. It does pain me to write about this, because this particular nurse had made such a positive impact on my life and treatment. Now I no longer have her as a part of my support system. Anyways, the center decided that it was necessary to transfer me to another facility or send me home due to my apparent slow or "lack of progress" and noncompliance with my treatment contract. I chose to go home since I felt like I was receiving conflicting information about my progress. Also, it did not make sense to transfer to another facility that had the same level of care.

Weightless

The night before leaving, my favorite night nurse came into my room to speak with me and say good-bye. She had mentioned that I had seemed different from my previous admission a few months prior; that in her eyes, I just "wasn't completely there" this time. I told her that this current admission had been significantly more difficult due to a multitude of factors. One of the factors that made it more difficult was tapering of the excessively high doses of the long-acting benzodiazepines. I was using that medication as an unhealthy emotion regulation coping skill. I had put more effort and willingness into this course of treatment than I ever had in the past, yet it was still not enough. Treatment no longer felt like a priority or even necessary after that fiasco. Belief that I will never be good enough confirmed.

What made leaving the treatment facility so difficult is that not only did I fail my own goals and expectations, but I felt like I had failed the nurses, the staff, the treatment team, and everyone else outside of the treatment bubble. I've had people tell me that I didn't fail treatment, treatment failed me. Honestly, I think it is a mix of both. What do you think? I found this written on a forum and it really resonated with me:

> "Clients are NEVER noncompliant. They may be fearful,
> overwhelmed, overburdened, nervous, traumatized,
> stressed, anxious. They may lack skills, time, finances,
> support, compassion, but they are never 'noncompliant'.
> DIG DEEPER, fellow health care practitioners!"
>
> **UNKNOWN**

Despite feeling like my treatment team deemed me "unwilling" or "noncompliant" or insert XYZ, I must give all of the staff at treatment facilities great praise. They have my immense respect. The environment they work in is very stressful. Many of the staff love the job they do. I do not believe that many of them receive the credit for all the hard work that they do. I suppose that staff doesn't always realize how much they impact the lives of the patients that live there for weeks or months. From most of my treatment admissions, I tend to associate myself with the nursing staff, and to rely on them more for support. Again, I do not believe they realize how much of a positive impact they can have on someone's life, especially during some of the most difficult times.

Of course, the nurses took care of my medical needs, administered my medications, talked me into accepting my NGT feeds and water flushes, but they also brought me joy, laughter, support, and compassion. Compassion was something I had been missing from my life for a very long time. The most recent admission has been the most impactful in regard to the support from the nurses.

One nurse would always play funny dog/animal videos while I received my bolus flushes (a method of tube feeding) because she knew those were one of my challenges. Another nurse would always come to check on me and talk to me if needed when I looked like I was going to cause trouble (which was basically always). I had many inside jokes with one nurse, especially about giving me a terrifying 600 ml fluid bolus. She was genuinely kind and encouraging during some of my hardest moments. And then there was my favorite day nurse, who was tough but actually really sweet, and somehow tolerated all of my shenanigans. I made her work for her money! I wish I could have gotten to work with her in real life, I think we would have made an excellent team.

Is it odd that I desperately desire to be empty, but at the same time hate the "empty" feeling that I have? I believe there are two different types of emptiness at play here. I want my body to be empty, clean, pure, yet I want the emptiness in my heart and my mind saturated. I think I use Ed to try and appease both types of emptiness, yet it never seems to last. Maybe this is why I find it difficult to leave treatment despite hating being in treatment. I form connections and enjoy joking around with the nurses, staff, and other patients. I think it fills some of that emptiness in my heart and my mind, and when I leave, that emptiness comes back. So, maybe in a backward way, returning to my Ed behaviors is a way to appease both types of that emptiness. It is just a theory.

EMPTINESS, A PROSE POEM

*There is a large gaping hole at the center of my chest. Its emptiness
is insatiable. The pain brings me down to my knees, where I
have to gasp for air and clasp my hands over my heart.*

*I try to fill that hole with pills and cutting, or starving and purging. The hole
shrinks for a little while, but it is a difficult wound to feed. It is greedy and
constantly wants more and more to lessen its emptiness, even for just a moment.*

*I tried to close that hole by suturing it together. I thought it would heal into a
pretty iridescent white straight scar, but I was wrong. Slowly, the wound began
to fester and ooze. It was no longer pearly white, but a red, inflamed, blistering
line that was beginning to open at the seams. Stitches popped off here and there,
leaving the wound uglier, angrier, hungrier, and more painful than before.*

*I thought, "How could this be?" When you close a wound, it's meant to heal,
not break back open worse than before. Unfortunately, this is no ordinary
wound. It is a wound of the heart, mind, and soul. Still, I repeatedly tried to
suture that hole closed only to end with the same result each time. I tried until
I was too weak to try anymore. Strength lost, body fragile, mind broken. The
wound consumes anything and everything. It will stop at nothing. And when
the victim has nothing left to give, it leaves its host, in search of a new one.*

JML

11

WHAT IS TREATMENT REALLY LIKE?

"Treatment ain't like burger king, you can't have it your way"

JESSICA LUNN

So, what is it really like to be a patient in Ed rehab or hospital? Now, before I bore you with the monotony of treatment, I have a few important things to point out.

One, treatment does not cure you as such. The point of going to treatment is to remove yourself from the crime scene. Treatment provides structure and support, and enforces accountability until you are able to manage your symptoms at a lower level of care. You must do the work for it to be effective. You cannot expect to enter a treatment facility, do whatever you want, ignore or fail to follow suggestions from your team, and then leave completely free of your disorder. In fact, being at a treatment center is easier than doing the work outpatient because you are basically living in a bubble. There are no distractions from the outside world (or they are at least limited), you have support from your peers and treatment team.

Two, treatment is equivalent to the most brutal bootcamp you will ever attend in your life. The tasks they expect of you feel unattainable or unachievable. Every aspect of yourself feels like it's severed apart from you and it is excruciating. If you have ever watched season four of the science fiction horror drama television series Stranger Things, think about how the villain Vecna attacks his victims. I'd say that is a pretty close description. As difficult as the whole process is, somewhere, somehow along the way, you begin to find your true self again. The demon's hold isn't as strong as it was, and the person you really are becomes the one in control. You begin to feel a spark of life again, you form special bonds with your fellow treatment community that are impossible to form anywhere else. There is an element of living, not just surviving.

Three, the logistics of treatment, insurance, and health care are all half ass backwards...and I say that nicely. This is a topic that deserves special attention, and indeed deserves its own book.

A DAY IN A TREATMENT CENTER

Okay folks, better buckle your seatbelt because we are going for a very unexciting ride! So, let's take a look at a fairly typical day in treatment. In general, most treatment centers that I have admitted to, despite having various treatment approaches, have a similar schedule and structure, with a few adjustments here and there.

Around 05:30-08:00 you wake up to get weighed and have your vitals checked (vital signs include respiration, heart rate or pulse, blood pressure, temperature and weight.) During this time, you shower and perform your morning hygiene routine and take your morning medications. If you had an NGT like I did, the nurse also checks that's in place for you to receive your tube feed. The dietitian determines how your feeds are ordered, and these are individually adjusted to each patient. For me, I would have breakfast and then remain on a continuous feed until approximately 8:00pm. Other patients were on continuous feeds like me, but the majority of patients with feeding tubes only got a tube feed if they did not complete their meal/snack or supplement. After morning medication is breakfast. Meal processing occurs after every meal but not snacks. Then it's group, morning snack, group, lunch, another one to two groups, then afternoon snack, group, then free time before dinner, and then more free time until bedtime snack. After snack the bathroom is open for night hygiene. Sounds fun, right?

Some places allow outside time at some point during the day if you are medically and psychiatrically stable. In between groups there is some free time to knit/crochet, do therapy homework, read, or play the very popular yet aggressive card game, Wahoo. Wahoo is a brutal card game similar to solitaire, except it is solitaire on steroids. Several people try to get rid of all their cards into one of the many solitaire piles. The goal is to do it as fast as possible, so they can receive an extra tally mark next to their name on the scoreboard. Sweating occurs (the Wahoo sweats), no apologies are allowed, and nothing said or done is taken personally. This game is serious business. One time I fell out of my wheelchair while playing a very intense, fast paced game, and everybody just looked at me and then kept playing! (They did ask if I was okay though). I was just mad that I lost my opportunity to put my card down!

No TV or music is allowed until all programming is over for the day, and some places now allow specific times for personal phone use (the one benefit of Covid).

Also, during the day, you are seen by the medical provider (frequency depends on your LOC, or level of care. The higher LOC, the more frequent you see providers). For me, I had to see the doctor every day due to being an inpatient. Regardless of whether you are inpatient or residential (IP or Res), you meet with your therapist two or three times per week, the dietitian once or twice a week, and your psychiatrist once or twice a week. If you are in a hospital setting, like ACUTE Center for Eating Disorders, the main focus is medical stabilization and weight restoration and other medical issues; there are no groups.

Treatment is highly structured on purpose, especially at the higher levels of care. It is easy for the Ed to sneak its way in and find control when there is less structure. Personally, I liked having structured days because it made the time go by faster and gave me something to do. Before almost every admission, I had a significant amount of unstructured free time (even when I was working full-time). This lack of structure ultimately led to worsening depression and increased Ed behaviors.

Everyone endures the monotony of treatment differently. Some days people's emotions are labile, other days the community is in an upbeat mood. It is difficult to tolerate the constantly changing vibe of the environment. In addition, new people coming in and patients leaving also drastically changes the community balance. For me, humor is the best medicine. I would much rather laugh about something than cry, although this coping skill can sometimes get me into trouble!

Since humor is my way of handling an unpleasant experience, I am usually the pranking nightmare of a patient. I may or may not have scared several nurses with fake roaches, placed googly-eyes all over the building, and started a running Mylanta tab on one of the nurse's credit cards. (Mylanta is the most frequent medicine given in treatment and is poured into a cup, so it is sometimes referred to as a "shot"!) I plead the fifth. I will however, confess to naming my feeding tube "Jake, from State Farm". Yes, he sounded hideous and wore khaki. Eventually I wrote a restraining order against him, but unfortunately the nurses vetoed me. It's okay though, I got a better lawyer and Jake had to say goodbye. Bye Jake!

WHAT ARE GROUPS LIKE?

I've mentioned group meetings and therapy, but, with so many groups scheduled, what are groups actually like? Sometimes the type of groups utilized is based on the treatment modalities of the treatment center. For example, one treatment center focused mainly on DBT or dialectical behavioral therapy, which focuses on teaching people coping strategies to help regulate their emotions and live a productive life. Other places focus more on CBT or cognitive behavioral therapy, which is widely used to help people solve problems, identify their beliefs, thoughts, and feelings, and regulate their behaviors accordingly. Some centers offer special treatment for co-occurring disorders such as depression, anxiety or substance abuse, or for trauma. (As a matter of fact, research indicates that the prospects for long-term recovery are better if any co-occurring disorders are treated together with the eating disorder.) So as you can see, groups vary widely, both in their intent and in the people who may attend.

In one group, we did visualization exercises and had to write a visualization of a safe place to imagine when anxiety is high or when struggling. This is what I wrote for my visualization exercise:

4/21/21:

I stood there at the top of a mountain in Peru. The air was warm with a cool breeze, bringing in that smell of fresh, clean air. As I stood there, I noticed I was surrounded by stunning mountains and had been standing under a bright shining sun. There were no clouds in the sky. Below me was the amazing and historic site of Machu Picchu. I had never felt so free and on top of the world. Every breathless and strenuous step I took towards the point of serenity was worth it. I could hear footsteps of the other tourists, but otherwise everything, including my mind and spirit, was quiet.—JML

Another example of a group I attended more recently focused on six words. We were given a word and then had to write down the first few thoughts we had related to the word. At first, I did not want to engage in this activity, but in the end, it actually gave me some insight. Here is what I wrote for those six words:

3/12/22:

1. *Peace*—Where to begin? What is it? I've only experienced a true state of peace through my ketamine treatments. The ketamine emptied my mind of all my worries so everything in my head felt quiet. To experience peace, you must experience pain. There is always a tradeoff.

2. *Wisdom*—It comes with experience. I feel as though I have gained indispensable wisdom from all of my years of suffering, and what I continue to go through.

3. *Secret*—Do you want to hear a secret? I have too many secrets. Holding onto them has left me a heavy load on

my shoulders. It has brought me down and made it nearly impossible to stand up sometimes. They haunt me day and night. Secrets are what keep us sick.

4. *Love*—This is all I have ever wanted. I wanted to feel validated, understood, and feel loved. It feels like I have a large void in my soul that has yet to be filled. Love can be a curse. There is always some element of pain or grief that goes along with it.

5. *Hope*—I've lost my hope, but I know someone out there is holding it for me. My candle is no longer burning bright, it has become a faint spark barely visible to the naked eye. I have been stripped by the hope I once had, but the light hasn't burnt out yet, so there is a chance that hope will one day be burning bright inside me.

6. *Connection*—I am about to lose some of the connection I have built here in treatment. I am being forced to discharge because I was unable to meet their standards. Connection is what I have craved for many years. Either I never got that connection or it was something I lost. The worst part is that it is usually due to my own mistakes. I do not want to go back to being alone, the loneliness is agonizing.—JML

12

RECOVERY VERSUS RECOVERED
OH, THE CONTROVERSY!

*Ed is a creature that clings to every crevasse. A savage that
climbs every mountain. A dementor that sucks out your soul. A
stab in the heart. A needle to a fraying thread. A blade to the
skin. Whether it is in the forefront of my mind or in the darkest,
smallest corner of my brain, it sits there and patiently waits for
every opportunity to rear its ugly head, strike, and gain control.
Until I die, it will always be there, waiting or controlling.*

JML

Recovery, in recovery, or recovered? Some individuals state that
full recovery from an Ed is possible, some say there is no such
thing because it is in the nature of an Ed to be lurking in the back-
ground, ever ready to spring back out again given the right combina-
tion of circumstances. The 12-step groups speak of the foe as being
"cunning, baffling and powerful", whether that relates to alcoholism
or to an eating disorder. Which side are you on? I think it is a difficult question to ask. Who even defines what recovery is or is not for

an individual? What's the difference between being in recovery versus being fully recovered? Again, this is an individualized answer. What recovery looks like for one person may look different for another person.

There is no official definition for recovery or recovered, but there is a generalized census as to what these terms mean:

- Recovery—the *process* of overcoming an Ed (or other addictive disorder).

- In recovery—the process by which someone *actively* chooses to overcome their Ed by *actively* making choices that support healthy behaviors and coping skills instead of their Ed.[42] For example, attending and engaging in treatment, addressing co-occurring issues, going to therapy, or following prescribed meal plan.

- Recover(ed)—free of Ed symptomatology, body acceptance, living not just surviving, finding yourself, creating a life outside of Ed (not focusing on weight, calories, numbers, exercise, food), and striving for health and happiness.[43]

If you have not already taken a guess, I am one of those individuals that does not believe "fully recovered" exists. This is just my point of view on the subject, it does not mean that those who do believe in full recovery are wrong or shouldn't have that opinion. Judgment-free zone here. It is a sensitive subject, but I will explain how I came to my conclusions about recovery. I like to think about it as being in remission rather than cured.

First, like many others, I believe that recovery is a never-ending process. Life is not black and white, and neither is recovery. There will be ups and downs in the process. Mistakes will be made and relapses may happen. You may find yourself in a situation at work, home, school, or anywhere that triggers old thoughts or behaviors. Recovery takes hard work every single day forever, because there will always be a new obstacle or change in your life. These challenges will test our resilience, and coping skills. They also allow us to practice using healthy tools that we have been taught, in tough times.[44]

Second, recover(ed) means that somewhere along the line there is an endpoint to self-discovery, living, and striving towards happiness and healthiness. Since when is there an end point to improving the quality of your life? Why would you prevent yourself from the continuous positive outcomes of constantly working on yourself? You are worth more than that! Give yourself credit for all the exceedingly difficult work you have done and keep going!

It's easy to get a little complacent about recovery when you are flourishing for a long period of time. You can never stop doing the work. In detox, all of the patients who had relapsed said it was because they had stopped doing the work. I've met people in treatment who've said that they were fully recovered from an Ed for 12+ years, yet there they were, sitting in a treatment center with me.

Keep choosing to fight another day, every day. And if you fall, get up off your arse! Don't stay on the ground. Let your battle scars give you the strength to keep fighting like the warrior that you are.

PART THREE

Living life to the fullest

THE DRAGONFLY

For I am a symbol of change, transformation, wisdom, and good luck.
I spent most of my life developing as larvae underwater.
Up to seventeen times,
I shed my outer covering, resulting in growth and maturity.
Each molting results in a new and stronger phase of life,
Until I am finally ready to go from the water straight into the air.
This process of molting can take up to five years.
Compared to the time I spend transforming underwater,
My life in the air is relatively short.
I get approximately six months to fly around the world.
Although my time is limited,
I have learned to live in the moment and make the most of my time.
For a human to transform like a dragonfly,
It is necessary to endure long periods of uncomfortable conditions,
Shed layer by layer to grow into a new phase of life,
And then fly like every day is their last.

JML

13

HOW TO COPE– NEW SKILLS

Live each day like a dragonfly!

10 LIFE LESSONS I'VE LEARNED

1. When you fall down, you stand back up even if it hurts like hell.

2. It doesn't matter how many times you fall.

3. You do not have to stand back up alone.

4. Nothing lasts forever; enjoy life's positive experiences to the fullest and allow yourself to fully grieve when life hands you loss.

5. There is always HOPE (Hold On Pain Ends).

6. If you do not have hope, then someone is holding it for you.

7. It's okay to not be okay.

8. It's okay to ask for help.

9. Every single person has the courage and strength to battle their demons

10. You are not given what you cannot handle and you will come out stronger in the end

COPING SKILLS

*"It is ok to lose your shit sometimes because if you keep your shit,
you'll end up full of shit and then you will explode and there'll
be shit everywhere. A shit storm. And nobody wants that".*

UNKNOWN

An intrinsic part of recovery is learning new skills to deal with every-day frustrations, instead of just coping, soldiering on, or losing our rag! If you're in a 12-step or other recovery group, or meeting regularly with a therapist, the chances are you'll be learning about these alternative skills and practicing as you go along. Here's a handy list for quick reference—feel free to take a sheet of paper or journal and fill in your own list!

Practical skills:

- Read a book

- Paint/art project/craft

- Journal

- Take a shower/bath

- Listen to music

- Crochet/knit

- Play an instrument

- Call a friend

- Paint your nails

- Play a board game or game on phone

- Watch a movie or tv show

- Gratitude journal

- Clean your room

- Play with your pet

- _____

- _____

- _____

- _____

Thinking skills

Sometimes practical activity isn't enough—you need to tackle your thinking as well. Here are a couple of helpful skills to use when (or ideally before) you feel challenged.

TIPP—this is a dialectical behavioral therapy (DBT) skill for distress tolerance. This is helpful when your anxiety or other emotion begins to feel distressing.[45] Do not wait to use this skill when you are having a full-blown panic attack. This is used to prevent you from getting there!!

- T—Temperature. Dip your face in cold water and hold it there for 30-60 seconds, to help slow heart rate and ease emotion. Do not attempt this if your cardiac function is compromised by your eating disorder or by other problems, and if you have any doubts, consult your doctor or health care professional.

- I—Intense exercise (good to get those endorphins flowing but HIGHLY NOT RECOMMENDED for those with eating disorders). Instead, go for a walk or practice some gentle yoga (again, consult your doctor if in doubt.)

- P—Paced breathing. Aim to slow your breathing down to five or six breaths a minute, so that each inbreath and out-breath together take 10 to 12 seconds. A timer or app can be helpful. If you feel yourself getting light-headed, desist.

- P—Progressive muscle relaxation. Go through all the muscles in your body, starting from the head and working your way down to your toes, alternately tensing and relaxing them.

HALT—This is a great skill for you to well, halt and determine what you are feeling physically and emotionally, and why. It stands for hungry, angry, lonely, and tired.[46]

- H—What am I hungry for?

- A—What am I angry about?

- L—What does loneliness bring up for me?

- T—What am I tired of?

14

HOW TO SUPPORT SOMEONE WITH AN EATING DISORDER

- First and foremost, make sure to take care of your own needs and adhere to your boundaries.

  » Remember, you cannot pour from an empty cup!

  » Also avoid blaming yourself. You did not cause this.

- Remember that eating disorders are not about food; food is just a symptom of the underlying issue (although prolonged, severe abstinence from food will bring about nutrition-related disorders).

- Be mindful about your own thoughts around food, dieting, and weight, especially commenting on your own body. Negative statements about yourself can trigger negative emotional responses in the person about their own body.

- Avoid making comments on body, weight, or looks. Instead make comments about the person. Example, "It is so nice to see your smile today!" or "I am proud of all of your hard work so far."

- Avoid making assumptions about their thoughts or feelings.

- Avoid comments such as, "You're too skinny, eat a burger", or, "Wow, that's a lot of food on your plate, are you going to eat all that?"

- Educate yourself about eating disorders. There are many resources online and in books (see below). Also be patient and show compassion toward your loved one.

- Instead of setting unrealistic goals, shaming, arguing, or blaming your loved one, focus on encouragement and hope. Remain positive during setbacks, and praise each positive step forward.

- Understand that recovery is a long-term journey. Recovery is not linear; slips, lapses, and relapses will happen, and the person should not be blamed. Encourage them to look on any lapses as a chance to learn, so they will be stronger in the future (see **Slip, lapse and relapse** below.)

- Ask how you can be of best support. For example, helping them stick to their meal plan, or taking them to their therapy sessions

- Validation is key! Set aside your own thoughts about what they are saying and don't try to fix anything or to jump in with solutions. Listening and validating their concerns goes a long way.

- Recognize and avoid enabling behaviors, such as organizing or restricting meals your own meals for dieting or social events around the person.

- Realize that if your loved one is acting out of character or behaving differently, it is the illness. Externalize the illness from your loved one.

- Encourage your loved one to seek extra support and offer support in that process. But make sure you are not their sole support.

- Use "I" statements (both parties here)—this makes the other person feel less defensive or like you are shaming/blaming them. For example:

  » "I feel concerned that you are falling back into your eating disorder behaviors," instead of, "You look like you are anorexic again."

  » "Mom, I do not feel supported when you talk about dieting around me," instead of, "You are just trying to sabotage my recovery efforts when you talk about dieting."[47,48]

15

SLIP, LAPSE, AND RELAPSE

A s mentioned above, recovery is not linear and individuals may go through slips, lapses or relapses. It is an expected part of recovery and is in fact useful in determining what areas still need to be worked on. The key to slips, lapses, and relapses is how you view it. Think of it as a learning opportunity rather than a failure. Instead of saying, "I blew it, I might as well go all out," try saying, "I slipped back into old behavior patterns, but I do not need to stay there—I now have new knowledge skills to help me move forward," or, 'This relapse shows me I still have something I need to work on in order to recover further—what is it?" or, "I know I can recover—I just need to tackle the last of the thought patterns that are holding me back." Beating yourself up is not going to be helpful, it is better to give yourself compassion when a slip occurs (you might like to revisit what I said about self-compassion earlier in this book in Part 2, **Empathy, compassion, and self-compassion**). Negative self-talk about a mistake in recovery may actually lead to further engagement of Ed behaviors. So, what is the difference between a slip, a lapse and relapse? Here is one set of definitions I have found helpful.

- Slip—an isolated incidence where someone engages in an Ed behavior.

  » Eg, skipped morning snack.

  » Person is able to remain in lower level of care and get back on track.

- Lapse—where a person has continuous slips over a short period of time.

  » Eg, skipped morning snack three times in one week and twice the next week.

  » Person can still maintain some recovery efforts as an outpatient, or may need to step up to a higher level of care or see their outpatient team more frequently.

- Relapse—when someone returns to full-blown eating disorder behaviors that last longer than a lapse.

  » It is very difficult to stop behaviors on their own and the person will likely need a higher level of care.[49]

UNCAGED

You will no longer own me,
I will not let you.
I am not a caged bird,
I choose to be free.

You hurt me,
Bruised me,
Battered me,
Took away my innocence,
And stole my soul,
But you will no longer own me.
I will remain free.

For years I let you tie me down,
Make me afraid, fear for my safety,
Tell me lies after lies,
But I will forgive you.

I do not forgive for your benefit,
But for mine,
Because resentment does not serve me.
It only keeps me trapped within your devious hold.

I will not give you that power.
You no longer own me.
I will remain an uncaged songbird
And sing a peaceful melody.

JML

HELPFUL BOOKS AND WEBSITES

BOOKS

- Costin, Carolyn, & Grabb, Gwen Schubert. (2012.) *8 Keys to Recovery from an Eating Disorder: Effective Strategies from Therapeutic Practice and Personal Experience*. W. W. Norton & Company.

- Fairburn, Christopher G. (2013). *Overcoming Binge Eating: The Proven Program to Learn Why You Binge and How You Can Stop* (2nd ed.). Guilford Press.

- Gaudiani, Jennifer L. (2018). *Sick Enough: A Guide to the Medical Complications of Eating Disorders*. Routledge.

- Johnston, Anita A. (2010). *Eating in the Light of the Moon: How Women Can Transform Their Relationship with Food Through Myths, Metaphors, and Storytelling*. Gurze Books.

- Schaefer, Jenni, & Rutledge, Thom. (2003). *Life Without Ed: How One Woman Declared Independence from Her Eating Disorder and How You Can Too*. McGraw-Hill.

- Scaefer, Jenni, (2009). *Goodbye Ed, Hello Me: Recover from Your Eating Disorder and Fall in Love with Life.* Mc-Graw-Hill.

- Tribole, Evelyn & Resch, Elyse. (2020). *Intuitive Eating, A Revolutionary Anti-diet approach (4th ed.).* Essentials.

- Tribole, Evelyn, & Resch, Elyse. (2017). *The Intuitive Eating Workbook: Ten Principles for Nourishing a Healthy Relationship with Food.* New Harbinger Publications.

- Matthew McKay, Matthew, Wood, Jeffrey C. & Brantley, Jeffrey Brantley. (2007). *The Dialectical Behavior Therapy Skills Workbook: Practical DBT Exercises for Learning Mindfulness, Interpersonal Effectiveness, Emotion Regulation, and Distress Tolerance.* New Harbinger Publications.

WEBSITES

Academy for Eating Disorders (AED)
https://www.aedweb.org/home

Alcoholics Anonymous
https://www.aa.org/

Alliance for Eating disorders—provides Ed information and a large database for treatment centers
https://www.allianceforeatingdisorders.com/

BetterHelp—provides online therapy services
https://www.betterhelp.com/

The Eating Disorder Foundation
https://eatingdisorderfoundation.org/

EdRefferal.com
http://edrefferal.com/

**Families Empowered and Supporting Treatment
of Eating Disorders (F.E.A.S.T)**
https://www.feast-ed.org/

National Alliance on Mental Illness (NAMI)
https://nami.org/

**National Association of Anorexia Nervosa and
Associated Eating Disorders (ANAD)**
https://anad.org/

National Eating Disorders Association (NEDA)
https://www.nationaleatingdisorders.org/

National Institute of Mental Health (NIMH)
https://www.nimh.nih.gov/

Overeaters Anonymous
https://oa.org/

ProjectHEAL—provides clinical assessments and diagnosis,
also has program for insurance navigation, treatment
placement with Identity Affirming Scholarships,
and cash assistance for high deductibles and copays
https://www.theprojectheal.org/

REFERENCES

1. Gaines, K. (2021). What is the nursing code of ethics? https://nurse.org/education/nursing -code-of-ethics/

2. Harvard, T.H. Chan. (2022). Economic costs of eating disorders report. https://www.hsph.harvard.edu/striped/report-economic-costs-of-eating-disorders/

3. ACUTE Center for Eating Disorders and Malnutrition (2020). Severe anorexia nervosa. https://www.acute.org/conditions/anorexia-nervosa

4. Mirror Mirror Eating Disorder Help. (2015). https://mirror-mirror.org/facts-staticstics/statistics -on-bulimia

5. Cowden, S. (2020). Diagnostic changes for eating disorders in the DSM-V. Verywellmind. https://www.verywellmind.com/diagnostic-changes-in-the-dsm-v-1138301

6. Machado, P. P., Grilo, C. M., & Crosby, R. D. (2017). Evaluation of the DSM-5 Severity Indicator for Anorexia Nervosa. *European eating disorders review: the journal of the Eating Disorders Association, 25*(3), 221–223. https://doi.org/10.1002/erv.2508

7. National Institute of Mental Health. (2021). Eating disorders. https://www.nimh.nih.gov/health/topics/eating-disorders

8. BEAT. (2022, October 8). Types of eating disorders. BEAT. https://www.beateatingdisorders.org.uk/get-information-and-support/about-eating-disorders/types/

9. Mulheim, L. (2020). Anosognosia and anorexia symptoms. Verywellmind. https://www.verywellmind.com/anosognosia-and-anorexia-3573545

10. Mulheim, L. (2020). Anosognosia and anorexia symptoms. Verywellmind. https://www.verywellmind.com/anosognosia-and-anorexia-3573545

11. Mehanna, H. M., Moledina, J., & Travis, J. (2008). Refeeding syndrome: what it is, and how to prevent and treat it. *BMJ (Clinical research ed.), 336*(7659), 1495–1498. https://doi.org/10.1136/bmj.a301

12. Biologywise. (n.d.). What is ATP. https://biologywise.com/what-is-atp

13. Mehanna, H. M., Moledina, J., & Travis, J. (2008). Refeeding syndrome: what it is, and how to prevent and treat it. *BMJ (Clinical research ed.), 336*(7659), 1495–1498. https://doi.org/10.1136/bmj.a301

14. ACUTE Center for Eating Disorders and Malnutrition (2021). Refeeding syndrome symptoms and warning signs. https://www.acute.org/resource/refeeding-syndrome-signs-symptoms

15. Johnson, T. (2022). The dangers and discomforts of eating disorder treatment: Refeeding syndrome, Pseudo Bartter Syndrome, and more. https://centerforchange.com/wp-content/uploads/Dangers-and-Discomforts-PP-handout.pdf

16. Gibson, D. (2022). Edema in eating disorder recovery: Causes, prevention, and treatment. https://www.acute.org/blog/edema-eating-disorder-recovery-causes-prevention-and-treatment

17. Collins Lyster-Mensh, L. (2020). The Minnesota starvation study: What does it mean for those with eating disorders? https://www.feast-ed.org/the-minnesota-starvation-study-what-does-it-mean-for-those-with-eating-disorders/

18. Rittenhouse, M. (2019). Genetics and anorexia nervosa—Anomalies on chromosome 12. https://www.eatingdisorderhope.com/blog/genetics-anorexia

19. University of North Carolina Health Care. (2017, May 12). For anorexia nervosa, researchers implicate genetic locus on chromosome 12: Powerful genomic study of anorexia nervosa conducted to date to identify the common roots anorexia shares with psychiatric, metabolic traits. *ScienceDaily*.

20. National Eating Disorders Association. (2022). Eating disorder myths. https://www.nationaleatingdisorders.org/toolkit/parent-toolkit/eating-disorder-myths

21. ANAD. (2022, October 8). Eating disorder statistics. ANAD. https://anad.org/eating-disorders-statistics/

22. Murray, S. B., Pila, E., Griffiths, S., & Le Grange, D. (2017). When illness severity and research dollars do not align: are we overlooking eating disorders?. *World psychiatry: official journal of the World Psychiatric Association (WPA)*, 16(3), 321. https://doi.org/10.1002/wps.20465

23. Substance Abuse and Mental Health Services Administration. (2022). HHS announces nearly $35 million to strengthen mental health support for children and young adults. https://www.samhsa.gov/newsroom/press-announcements/20220309/hhs-announces-35-million-strengthen-mental-health

24. Murray, S. B., Pila, E., Griffiths, S., & Le Grange, D. (2017). When illness severity and research dollars do not align: are we overlooking eating disorders?. *World psychiatry: official journal of the World Psychiatric Association (WPA)*, 16(3), 321. https://doi.org/10.1002/wps.20465

25. Murray, S. B., Pila, E., Griffiths, S., & Le Grange, D. (2017). When illness severity and research dollars do not align: are we overlooking eating disorders?. *World psychiatry: official journal of the World Psychiatric Association (WPA)*, 16(3), 321. https://doi.org/10.1002/wps.20465

26. ANAD. (2022, October 8). Eating disorder statistics. ANAD. https://anad.org/eating-disorders-statistics/

27. National Eating Disorders Association. (2022). Eating disorder myths. https://www.nationaleatingdisorders.org/toolkit/parent-toolkit/eating-disorder-myths

28. Live Another Day. (2022, October 8). Co-occurring eating disorders and substance abuse. https://liveanotherday.org/co-occurring-disorders/eating-disorders/

29. National Eating Disorder Association. (2022). Eating disorders in men and boys. https://www.nationaleatingdisorders.org/learn/general-information/research-on-males#:~:text=Despite%20the%20stereotype%20that%20eating%20disorders%20only%20occur,common%20among%20men%20as%20they%20are%20among%20women

30. National Eating Disorders Association. (2022). Eating disorder myths. https://www.nationaleatingdisorders.org/toolkit/parent-toolkit/eating-disorder-myths

31. Dough, J. (2018). It's time to debunk these 6 eating disorder myths. https://themighty.com/topic/eating-disorders/debunking-myths-about-eating-disorders#1:%20All%20eating%20disorder%20patients%20look%20sick.,doctors%20and%20dentists%20can%20miss%20certain%20warning%20signs

32. Hall, M., & Hall, S. (2016). Managing the psychological impact of medical trauma: A guide for mental health and healthcare professionals. https//:doi.org/10.1891/9780826128942

33. Barbash, E. (2017). Different types of trauma: Small 't' versus large 't'. https://www.psychologytoday.com/us/blog/trauma-and-hope/201703/different-types-trauma-small-t-versus-large-t

34. Blanchfield, T. (2022). What is medical trauma? Verywellmind. https://www.verywellmind.com/what-is-medical-trauma-5211358

35. Hall, M., & Hall, S. (2016). Managing the psychological impact of medical trauma: A guide for mental health and healthcare professionals. https//:doi.org/10.1891/9780826128942

36. Waichler, I. (2022). Medical trauma: Effects, treatments, and how to cope. https://www.choosingtherapy.com/medical-trauma/

37. Compassion International. (2022). Understanding the meaning of compassion. https://www.compassion.com/child-development/meaning-of-compassion/

38. Robbins, T. (2022, October 8) A guide to empathy and compassion: The difference between empathy and compassion- and why we need both. https://www.tonyrobbins.com/mind-meaning/compassion-vs-empathy/

39. Neff, K. (2022, October 8). Definition and three elements of compassion. https://self-compassion.org/the-three-elements-of-self-compassion-2/

40. Comninos, A. (2022, October 8). The benefits of self-compassion. Mindfulness and clinical psychology solutions. https://mi-psych.com.au/the-benefits-of-self-compassion/#:~:text=Benefits%20of%20Self-Compassion%3A%20Research%20Findings%201%20Strongly%20predictive,intimate%2C%20are%20more%20giving%2C%20and%20are%20less%20controlling

41. Comninos, A. (2022, October 8). The benefits of self-compassion. Mindfulness and clinical psychology solutions. https://mi-psych.com.au/the-benefits-of-self-compassion/#:~:text=Benefits%20of%20Self-Compassion%3A%20Research%20Findings%201%20Strongly%20predictive,intimate%2C%20are%20more%20giving%2C%20and%20are%20less%20controlling

42. Hunnicutt, C. (2022, October 8). Fully recovered vs. in recovery: A discussion of the similarities and differences. Monte Nido. https://www.montenido.com/fully-recovered-vs-in-recovery/

43. Doeblin, A. (2016). What does it mean to recover from an eating disorder? https://recovery-warriors.com/what-it-means-to-recover-from-an-eating-disorder/

44. ANAD. (2022, October 8). Words are a powerful thing: Recovered vs. recovery. ANAD. https://anad.org/recovered-vs-recovery/

45. Rosenthal, J. (2022). Dialectical behavioral therapy distress tolerance skills: TIPP skills. Manhattan psychology group. https://manhattanpsychologygroup.com/dbt-tipp-skills/

46. Cleveland Clinic. (2022). HALT: Pay attention to these four stressors on your recovery. Health Essentials. https://health.clevelandclinic.org/halt-hungry-angry-lonely-tired/

Weightless

47. Snapclarity. (2019). 5 tips on how to support someone with an eating disorder. Medium. https://medium. com/snapclarity/5-tips-on-how-to-support-someone-with-an-eating-disorder-b53ed9e624c8

48. BEAT. (2022, October 8). Supporting someone with an eating disorder. BEAT. https:// www.beateatingdisorders.org.uk/get-information-and-support/support-someone-else/ tips-for-supporting-somebody-with-an-eating-disorder/

49. Derrick, A. (2019). Eating disorder relapse is common. Eating Recovery Center. https://www. eatingrecoverycenter.com/blog/recovery/Eating-Disorder-Relapse-is-Common

Made in the USA
Las Vegas, NV
23 December 2024

15242284R00080